MILITARY HISTORY
OF NEW JERSEY

MILITARY HISTORY
OF NEW JERSEY

DAVID PETRIELLO

Foreword by Mark Edward Lender

Charleston · London

THE
History
PRESS

Published by The History Press
Charleston, SC 29403
www.historypress.net

First published 2014

Manufactured in the United States

ISBN 978.1.62619.627.8

Library of Congress CIP data applied for.

CONTENTS

Foreword, by Mark Edward Lender   7
Introduction   11

1. Conquering the Delaware and the Hudson: The Military History
   of New Netherlands and New Sweden   13
2. New Jersey in the Wars of Empire:
   Colonial New Jersey's Military History   33
3. Crossroads of the Revolution:
   New Jersey and the Fight for Independence   65
4. From Little Turtle to Tecumseh:
   New Jersey and the Wars of the Early Republic   93
5. From the Halls of Montezuma to the Shores
   of New Jersey: New Jersey and Manifest Destiny   109
6. Twice Against Lincoln: The Civil War in New Jersey   117
7. New Jersey and the USS *Maine*:
   The Garden State in the Age of Imperialism   133
8. Sabotage and Submarines:
   New Jersey and the Great War   143
9. Against the Axis: New Jersey in World War II   157
10. Cold War along the Hot Shore: New Jersey and the
    Wars of Modernity   167

Notes   179
Index   187
About the Author   191

FOREWORD

You may not be interested in war, but war is interested in you." This famous quotation is mistakenly attributed to Bolshevik revolutionary Leon Trotsky, but even if Trotsky never said it, the words carry a simple but powerful truth. Conflict—war, if you will—has been part of the human experience since time immemorial, and as distasteful as we may find it, it will be into the foreseeable future. We would do well to try to understand it. When, how and why has war occurred in given times and places, and what results have followed? These are important questions, for, like it or not, war has touched on most aspects of every modern society. To varying degrees, military affairs or concerns have become woven into our political, cultural, economic, scientific, technological and even spiritual lives. Certainly this has been true in America. Before European colonization, warfare was endemic among many Indian tribes; the act of colonization itself, as historian James Axtell has reminded us, was an invasion of massive proportions. Even the slave trade dealt with captives taken by war and other violent means in Africa, and slavery required organized military efforts to maintain in America. The independence, expansion and internal and external relations of the United States have been fraught with conflicts large and small. As Americans, war indeed has been "interested" in us.

The same has been true of New Jersey. The state has served, as one historian has put it, as a "mirror on America"; important events and trends generally have had a reflection in New Jersey history, and military developments have been no exception. In this volume, David Petriello makes this abundantly clear. As he convincingly demonstrates, New Jersey has been a "mirror" on America's military history.

Petriello's approach is chronological. His book is a useful survey of New Jersey's participation in America's conflicts, and it details how frequently residents of the Garden State have been caught up in military operations. From the colonial era to the present, New Jersey has sent its sons and daughters to serve in virtually every conflict in American history. There was plenty of fighting in early New Jersey (or in what became New Jersey); the Lenape, the Dutch, the Swedes and the British were all involved. During the colonial wars, New Jersey troops fought in far-flung theaters against the French, the Spanish and the Indians. The War for Independence saw more fighting in New Jersey than in any of the other colonies. After the Revolution, the state sent most of its sons and daughters to war in regions far from home, and the author follows them as they followed the colors through the campaigns of the War of 1812, the Mexican War the carnage of the Civil War and many others. Petriello covers all this in a clear narrative and brings the story into the modern era, noting the active naval operations off the New Jersey shore during World War II and the participation of Garden State soldiers, sailors and air crew in the conflicts of our own generation, including the war on terror. The author has given us a short but comprehensive volume.

To his credit, Petriello takes the time to remind us of some of the lesser-known chapters in state military history. He rightly points out that the land riots of the 1740s were, in fact, military in character. While disorganized and resorting to highly irregular mob actions, furious yeomen took up arms against court proceedings threatening their land titles. Then there was the extraordinary skirmishing between Jerseymen and New Yorkers disputing the colonial boundaries; it may have been the only combat in history in which rivals hurled pumpkins at one another. Petriello knows how to pick an anecdote.

War, however, is about much more than fighting. In reading Petriello's survey, another quote—actually an old army aphorism—comes to mind: "Amateurs talk tactics; professionals talk logistics." That is, without the sinews of war—supplies, food, weapons, munitions, equipment and the means to move and distribute them—sustained combat is usually impossible, even in guerrilla warfare. Although not a battlefield after the Revolution, New Jersey remained a key element in the nation's military affairs. From the 1700s to the present, the state has hosted significant munitions manufacturing operations; defense research and development; training, communications and transportation facilities; coastal and air defense installations; and an industrial base with broad applications to military affairs—the "military-industrial complex," if you will. Again to his credit, Petriello does not scant this important aspect of the story.

It is a truism that every generation writes its own history. It has been over thirty years since any historian has attempted a general survey of the military in New Jersey (I ought to know—I wrote the last one), and it is past time for a new one. David Petriello has given us a good one.

MARK EDWARD LENDER
Kean University, *Emeritus*

INTRODUCTION

E very schoolchild in New Jersey learns at some point that the state was the "crossroads of the American Revolution." Washington's crossing of the Delaware and the subsequent Battle of Trenton figures largely not only in state lore but also in American history in general. Engagements at Morristown and Monmouth are perhaps less well known outside the state but are still extensively taught in schools from Bergen County to Cape May. Yet even within the Garden State, New Jersey's involvement in other conflicts, both on its own soil and abroad, are less well known to the point of even being ignored. The state's military history has been largely subsumed by that of the nation, ignoring the sacrifices and achievements of those within New Jersey. On the academic level, many fine scholarly works exist on New Jersey in the American Revolution, and a number have been written on its role in the Civil War as well. Yet little to no extensive research has been done on the experiences of New Jersey and its citizens during the numerous other conflicts that raged during its 350 years of existence. This work was written to address that disparity. A state as old, diverse and historically and militarily important as New Jersey deserves a comprehensive study of its military history.

Finally, in order to be as comprehensive as possible, this work will also examine the impact of the various wars of the state's history on those citizens who did not serve, which has always been a much larger percentage. The farmers, factory workers, nurses, drivers, sailors, writers and taxpayers of the state were as vital to victory as the men in the field. Thus, their story needs to be told as well.

CHAPTER 1

CONQUERING THE DELAWARE AND THE HUDSON: THE MILITARY HISTORY OF NEW NETHERLANDS AND NEW SWEDEN

The importance of the area that would become New Jersey can be attested to through the numerous conflicts fought on its soil. Occupying a moderate climate zone along the coast, controlling access to two major river systems and being situated between the various Northern and Southern Colonies, the area of the future Garden State proved desirable to many different groups. Due to this, the first century and a half of New Jersey's existence as a European colony was hardly a time of peace. Confrontation with native inhabitants, competition among the European powers themselves and local instability all contributed to numerous military episodes that ravaged the area. In fact, this era would see the most battles to occur on the state's soil apart from the Revolutionary War years.

PRE-COLUMBIAN CONFLICT

Europeans were not the first to bring violence and war to the region. The Lenape, or Delaware, an Algonquin tribe who inhabited the environs of New Jersey and eastern Pennsylvania before the arrival of the Europeans, had numerous tales and legends about battles that were both mythical and historical. One of these involved the Yah-qua-whee, a word that has been translated as either "monster" or "mastodon." According to the Delaware, the Great Spirit placed the Yah-qua-whee on the earth to benefit the

Depiction of Susquehannock Indians with a battle between tribes in the background. *Library of Congress.*

natives, but they instead became destructive, making war against both man and the other animals. "It was fierce, powerful, and invincible, its skin… so strong and hard that the sharpest spears and arrows could scarcely penetrate it."[1] A fierce battle ensued, in which the other animals, both great and small, fought the monsters. The hills, mountains and forests became devastated, but in the end, thanks to the ferocity of the animals and the lightning bolts of the Great Spirit, the Yah-qua-whee were defeated. Their own weight drowned them amid the muck and blood of the battlefield, with their great bones occasionally being discovered by the natives years later. The Great Spirit would compensate man by causing cranberries to grow among the marshes and bogs, representing both the muck and blood of the battle and producing life from death.[2]

The early Indians of the region themselves proved to be no less warlike than the monsters inhabiting their woodlands. While evidence is scarce

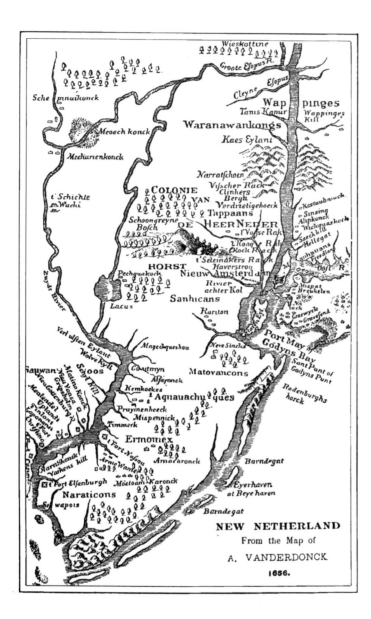

A map of the native tribes of New Jersey as of 1656. *From King's* Handbook of New York City: 1893.

of defensive works built around the villages of the Lenape, historians have been able to prove the existence of palisades around the settlements of the Susquehannock, an Iroquoian speaking people.[3] These people, an enemy of the Lenape, were also known to have built numerous forts throughout the eastern Pennsylvania region, constructions that would have been unnecessary in a peaceful environment.[4] The Swedes and Dutch would eventually refer to the Susquehannock people as the Minqua, a derivative of the Lenape term for them, which translates as "treacherous." Well into the colonial period, the Minqua were reported by the Europeans as viciously waging war against the other tribes of the area. In his journal, David de Vries noted that fugitive natives he met in 1633 claimed that the Minqua "had killed about ninety men of the Sankiekans."[5] Delaware legends tell of a time before the arrival of Europeans during which long wars were fought with the six Iroquois nations. "But the former were always too powerful for the Six Nations. The latter were convinced that if they continued the wars, their total extirpation would be inevitable."[6]

Yet at the same time, rivalries existed as well within the various groups. The Sankhikan, who inhabited the central part of New Jersey, were known to be deadly enemies of the Manhattan tribe, both of whom were Lenape people. An excavation at Tottenville on Staten Island in 1895 uncovered the remains of three pre-Columbian skeletons. All gave evidence of having been executed, with the group being pierced over twenty-three times by arrows of differing compositions.[7] New Jersey was the site of internal conflict for hundreds of years and was a border region in the long-standing rivalry between the Iroquois and Algonquin people, a role it would again play with the arrival of various European powers.

DUTCH AND SWEDES AT WAR

The first major exploration of the region by Europeans proved to be a harbinger of the further conflict that was to follow. In 1609, Henry Hudson, sailing aboard the *Half Moon*, skirted the coastline of New Jersey exploring the region for the Netherlands. Measuring around eighty-five feet in length and carrying only sixteen intrepid men, the vessel was hardly an overpowering warship. As Hudson rounded Sandy Hook and approached modern-day Keansburg, he dispatched a sixteen-foot shallop with five men aboard to explore the area of the Kill Van Kull and Newark Bay. As the men sailed through the area, they were approached by two large canoes, each twenty feet in length and carrying a total of twenty-six natives. From the accounts delivered later by the men, it appears that the encounter quickly turned violent. Robert Juet, a member of Hudson's crew, recorded in his journal what took place:

> So they went in two leagues and saw an open Sea, and returned; and as they came back they were set upon by two Canoes, the one having twelve, the other fourteen men. The night came on, and it began to rain, so that their Match went out; and they had one man slain in the fight, which was an English-man named John Colman, with an Arrow shot into his throat, and two more hurt.[8]

The natives unleashed their arrows on the crewmen in the boat, beginning a small battle that ended with their retreat after the Dutch returned fire. The four other crew members returned the body of their deceased comrade to Hudson the next morning after a difficult and fearful night on the water. The explorer subsequently ordered his body to be buried ashore at what became known as Colman's Point in modern-day Keansburg. No further attacks occurred, and the *Half Moon* continued on its way to discover what would become New York City.

The first battle to take place in New Jersey has been commemorated in numerous ways over the past four centuries. The scene has been memorialized in a mural on the walls of the Hudson County Courthouse, depicting the first recorded murder in the state.

Likewise, poet Thomas Frost paid homage to the battle and Colman in a poem first published in 1908:

> And suddenly our unshaped dread
> Took direful form and sound.
> For from a near nook's rocky shade,
> Swift as pursuing hound,
> A savage shallop sped, to hold
> From stranger feet that strand of gold.
>
> And rageful cries disturbed the peace
> That on the waters slept;
> And Echo whispered on the hills,
> As though an army crept,
> With flinty axe and brutal blade,
> Through the imperforate forest shade.

The arrival of Henry Hudson in New Jersey. *Gilder Lehrman Collection.*

> *"What! are ye cravens?"* Colman said;
> *For each had shipped his oar.*
> *He waved the flag: "For Netherland,*
> *Pull for yon jutting shore!"*
> *Then prone he fell within the boat,*
> *A flinthead arrow through his throat!* [9]

Seven years after the Dutch established New Amsterdam, Captain Cornelius Jacobsen Mey, the namesake of Cape May, built Fort Nassau at the mouth of Big Timber Creek near Red Bank in Gloucester County. Erected in 1623, this was perhaps the first European settlement on the eastern bank of the Delaware River. Yet the fortress proved to be anything but secure. While exploring the area during the winter of 1630–31, David de Vries reported finding the stronghold abandoned, its ruins inhabited by natives. Local Indians who had ostensibly gathered to trade even attempted to attack de Vries and his crew, though luckily for the Dutch captain, he was warned by a friendly native woman.

The previous year, a similar situation had unfolded at the Dutch settlement of Swanendael. In his journal, de Vries claims that an argument had erupted between the Dutch commander of the settlement and the Minquas after one of the latter had stolen the company's metal coat of arms to make into a pipe. The natives, angered after the exchange, returned later and butchered the Dutch as they worked in the fields.

> *In descending the stairs one of the Indians seized an axe and cleft his head so that he fell down dead. They also relieved the sick man of life, and shot into the dog, who was chained fast, and whom they most feared, twenty-five arrows before they could dispatch him. They then proceeded towards the rest of the men, who were at work, and, going amongst them with pretensions of friendship, struck them down. Thus was our young colony destroyed.*[10]

By the time their bloody business was done, thirty-two Dutch lay dead in the settlement. De Vries would describe the scene as follows: "It was almost burnt up. Found lying here and there [were] the skulls and bones of our people, and the heads of the horses and cows which they had brought with them."[11]

The natives of northern and central New Jersey and the surrounding regions would continue to be a problem for a generation. Johan Printz of New Sweden once famously said, "Nothing would be better than that a couple hundred soldiers should be sent here and kept here until we broke the necks of all of them in the river."[12] Yet the Indians of South Jersey largely avoided fighting the Europeans. This internal pacifism when combined with the neighboring, buffering colonies of Pennsylvania and New York did much to isolate most of New Jersey from the frontier wars and Indian raids characteristic of the Middle Colonies.

In fact, the vast majority of all battles to be fought in the Garden State during this time period occurred between European nations. In 1635, a decade after the establishment of the Dutch along the Delaware, a group of English settlers from Connecticut attempted to take Fort Nassau during one of its unoccupied periods. Wouter van Twiller, the director general of New Netherlands, had already lost the Connecticut Valley to English settlers and therefore moved decisively to counter this new threat to the Dutch colonial empire in America. The fort was quickly retaken, and David de Vries brought the thirteen to fourteen English prisoners back to New Amsterdam, where they were eventually sent back to the

Connecticut colony from which they had come. New Jersey was again safely under Dutch control, but this situation was to last for only a few short years.

Another failed settlement attempt by the English under Sir Edmund Plowden during the 1640s was paralleled by a more successful expedition by the Swedes. In March 1638, Peter Minuit, formerly of the Dutch East India Company, sailed with two ships up the Zuydt Riviere, as the Dutch referred to the Delaware River. His two ships, the *Kalmar Nyckel* and the *Fogel Grip*, with twenty-six men aboard from various nations, were tasked with establishing a fort and trading post for the queen of Sweden. Minuit moved two miles up the Minquas Kill, or Christina River, firing off his cannons to claim the area.

The *Grip*, after partaking in a failed trade mission to the English settlement of Jamestown, sailed upriver toward the Dutch fort at Timber Creek. Challenged by the garrison at Fort Nassau, the ship eventually retreated back down the Delaware. Realizing that the Swedish claim had to be secured, Minuit began the construction of Fort Christina at modern-day Wilmington, Delaware. The fort was a square structure containing two log buildings, a storehouse and a dwelling. Though Minuit armed the bastion with the cannon from the *Kalmar Nyckel*, an uneasy peace was maintained between the Swedes and the Dutch for the next few years.

The first serious challenge to both parties in the area came again from English expansion into New Jersey. Seven years after Britain's first attempt to infiltrate the area, a second expedition sent from New Haven Colony set up trading posts at the Schuylkill and Varken's Kill, modern-day Salem Creek, in 1642. These settlements further strained the fur trade for both the Dutch and Swedish. In response, Governor Kieft of New Netherlands proposed a joint task force be sent to drive the English out. In accordance with this, Jan van Ilpendam was dispatched from Fort Nassau with twenty men and two yachts. The English refused to leave, and Van Ilpendam resorted to force to remove them from the area. The settlement at Salem was broken up and reduced to ashes. The English had again been driven from New Jersey.

Kieft's War

The first major war to be fought in New Jersey erupted soon after the expulsion of the English. William Kieft, the leader behind that move, had arrived in New Netherlands in 1638. He was in charge of a small yet potentially profitable colony of about eight hundred souls. Starting in 1630, the Dutch inhabitants of Manhattan had also been spilling over into modern-day Hudson County, establishing the patroonship of Pavonia. Kieft's dealings with the natives soon turned antagonistic. Attempts by the governor to extract tribute from the tribes failed and only strained relations further. The theft of some pigs from the farm of David de Vries ultimately became the *cause de célèbre* that allowed Kieft to launch a punitive raid against a Raritan village on Staten Island. The Raritans, in return, would burn de Vries's house and kill four of his workers.

Murder followed murder as the situation slowly escalated. A local Dutchman, Claes Swits Rademacher, was murdered with an axe by a Wappinger in 1641. That same year, a drunken brawl turned violent between Hackensack Indians and some Dutch colonists at AchterKol along the present-day Hackensack River. Fear among the residents led to the formation of a council of twelve to deal with the impending crisis.

Kieft soon took matters into his own hands, launching a punitive expedition against the natives in 1642. Unfortunately for the Dutch, the force got lost in the dark. A second expedition sent later would fare no better. Anger began to mount against the governor due to his perceived inaction in the matter, "keeping himself protected in a good fort, out of which he had not slept."[13] In response to both local criticism as well as his own ideas concerning the natives, Kieft launched an all-out war against the Indians of New York and New Jersey in early 1643.

On February 26, 1643, a party of eighty Dutch soldiers under Sergeant Rodolf entered an Indian refugee camp in Pavonia, Jersey City. The Weckquaesgeek and Tappan had sought protection at the Dutch settlement following attacks by their traditional enemies, the Mahican. Falling upon the helpless natives, the Dutch massacred over eighty men, women and children. David de Vries, who opposed the move by the governor, wrote years later that "about midnight I heard a great shrieking and went to the ramparts of the fort and I looked over to Pavonia, and saw nothing but firing and heard the shrieks of the savages being murdered in their sleep."[14] Their bodies were thrown into trenches, and those who escaped fled to New Amsterdam thinking their assailants to be Mahican.

> *Infants were torn from their mothers' breasts, and hacked to pieces in the presence of their parents, and pieces thrown into the fire and in the water, and other sucklings, being bound to small boards, were cut, stuck, and pierced, and miserably massacred in a manner to move a heart of stone. Some were thrown into the river, and when the fathers and mothers endeavored to save them, the soldiers would not let them come on land but made both parents and children drown...some came to our people in the country with their hands, some with their legs cut off, and some holding their entrails in their arms.*[15]

That same night at Corler's Hook, on the Lower East Side, an additional forty natives were killed by a Dutch party under Maryn Adriansen. Traditional accounts relate how the soldiers returned some of the heads to Manhattan to use as kickballs in the streets of the city. De Vries and many Dutch were appalled by the action: "Did the Duke of Alva in the Netherlands ever do anything more cruel?"[16]

Yet the Indians did not differentiate between those who supported and those who despised the actions of Kieft, and a general war soon ensued. The natives began to raid Dutch settlements throughout the area, including in Hoboken, where the house of Aert Teunissen was attacked and his family slaughtered. Aert himself, who had constructed the first brewery in New Jersey, was later killed on his boat in Shrewsbury Inlet. Vriensendael, the first Dutch settlement in Bergen County, was likewise raided with almost all homes destroyed except that of David de Vries due to his high standing among the natives. The Indians did take a copper kettle from him to melt for arrowheads, but they spared his brewery. These attacks died down after a few months but resumed with the onset of summer.

The natives next appeared in the Achter Col region around Newark Bay and proceeded to raid and burn the settlement, allowing only a handful of soldiers and boys to escape in a canoe. As a colonist reported at the time, "The Indians swarm in that district and burn and slay whatever they come across."[17] On October 1, the Indians lured Jacob Stoffelsen out of the Van Vorst farm and proceeded to slaughter or capture the other inhabitants inside. Finally, an attack on the boweries of Pavonia was staved off only due to the presence of two ships of war and

Re-creation of the Pavonia Massacre by students of PS 11 in Jersey City. *Jersey City Public Library.*

a privateer. Though much of the grain and cattle was saved, the natives still burned most of the buildings after lighting the thatched roofs on fire. An army of 1,500 Algonquins ravaged New Netherlands, and few settlements were spared. Anne Hutchinson, having famously fled from persecution in Massachusetts Bay, had settled with her family in the area of present-day Bronx, New York. Yet neither her good relations with the Narragansett Indians of Rhode Island nor her storied determination saved her and her family from being scalped and killed in a war that they probably knew little about.

The Dutch went on the offensive in the winter, killing an estimated five hundred Weckquaesgeek. Captain John Underhill, famous for massacring Pequot men, women and children at Mystic in 1637, was hired by the Dutch and proceeded to kill hundreds of natives in 1644. Yet the death and destruction caused by Kieft's war sparked furor among the Dutch. Two separate attempts were made on the life of the governor. The first, by Maryn Adriansen, failed when a councilor jumped at the assassin and shoved his thumb under the gun's hammer, while the second attempt by

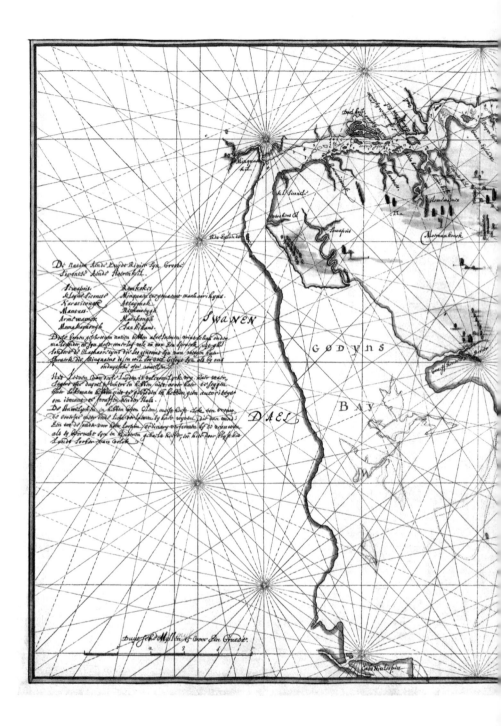

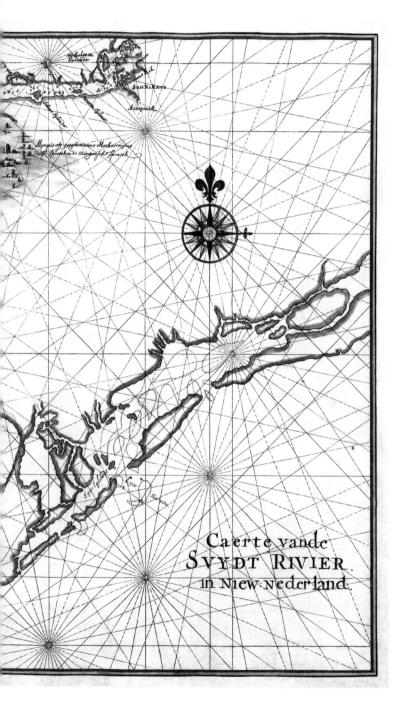

A map of fortifications and settlements along the Delaware as of 1639. *Library of Congress.*

Jacob Slangh resulted in the attacker being shot and his head placed on a pike outside New Amsterdam. The war would eventually grind to a halt by 1645 with a truce being signed between both sides. Little was achieved except death and the weakening of both sides.

EXPANSION OF NEW SWEDEN

While the Dutch were fighting for their survival in northeastern New Jersey and New York, the Swedes were taking the opportunity to expand along the Delaware. The leader behind this movement was Johan Printz, the four-hundred-pound new governor of New Sweden, referred to as "Big Belly" by the local natives. The Swedes began to construct forts throughout the region, bypassing the various Dutch positions. In May 1643, Fort NyaElfsborg was erected between the Salem River and Alloway Creek. From its high vantage point, the Swedes could control access to the Delaware River. All Dutch ships were forced to stop before the fort, with even the famed David de Vries being required to strike his colors on a trip up the river at the end of the year. Unfortunately, the inhospitable terrain and sheer number of mosquitoes present there led the Swedes to dub the bastion Myggenborg, or "Mosquito Castle." That same year, construction also began on a massive fort on Tinicum Island called Fort NyaGothenborg. Built to command both the Delaware and Schuylkill Rivers, the settlement became the new capital of the colony.

The high point for the Swedes came in June 1643 when two colonists approached Governor Printz with a dreadful story. George Lamberton, one of the English who had settled at Salem Creek in 1642, was actively attempting to bribe the natives to rise up and murder the Dutch and Swedes in the region. Printz acted decisively, sending spies to gather more intelligence on Lamberton's plans. Once accurate information was gathered, the Englishman himself was tricked into coming to Fort Christina, at which point he was arrested, imprisoned and placed on trial. After being found guilty, he was deported back to New Haven Colony.[18] Printz had again asserted Swedish claims to the area of New Jersey.

Dutch-Swedish War

Though the Dutch and Swedes had generally lived together in harmony along the Delaware, with the expulsion of the English and the tightening of the fur market, relations worsened. Printz inaugurated the conflict by refusing Dutch ships the right to trade down the river. This was soon followed by the limiting of the ability of traders from Fort Nassau to hunt for minerals in the region. Finally, the arms of the Dutch West India Company were stripped from Swedish settlements.

The Dutch under the famous Stuyvesant responded by building their own fort to control the Schuylkill. Constructed in 1648, Fort Beversreede quickly became a source of contention for the Swedes. In response, Governor Printz sent a detachment of soldiers to cut down trees in front of the fort and destroy fruit-bearing trees in the region. When this show of force failed, the Swedes next took to building a blockhouse between Fort Beversreede and the river. This new structure, Fort NyaKorsholm, frustrated Dutch efforts to control the land and its trade routes. Fort Beversreede, thus rendered useless, would finally be abandoned, after much vandalism by the Swedes, in 1650.

Stuyvesant soon stepped up his efforts to expel the Swedes. In May 1651, an armed Dutch ship was sighted off the coast of Cape May "with cannon and people well armed."[19] This show of force was followed a year later by a full assault launched by the governor general of New Netherlands. In late June 1651, Stuyvesant appeared at Fort Nassau after marching across the breadth of New Jersey. His 120 men met up with a naval force at the fortress and prepared to attack the Swedish positions. Yet the numerical weakness of the Dutch force prevented a full assault. Stuyvesant instead settled for sailing up and down the length of the river, drums sounding and cannon thundering, in an attempt to intimidate the Swedes into submission. Printz responded rather mockingly by sailing in his own yacht behind the Dutch force, copying their performance.

The Dutch next decided to follow the lead of the Swedes by leapfrogging Fort Christina and establishing their own fortified post farther down the Delaware River at what is now New Castle, Delaware. Fort Casimir, as it was christened, replaced the old Dutch position at Fort Nassau, which was subsequently razed.[20] Yet this cold war of positioning quickly heated up with the taking of Fort Casimir by the Swedes in May 1654 under the new governor, Johan Rising. The under-

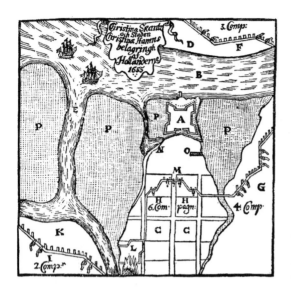

A drawing of the Battle of Fort Christina. *From Justin Winsor's* Narrative and Critical History of America, *Vol. 4 (1884).*

defended position fell "without force or hostility" and was renamed Fort Trinity for the day of its capture.

Stuyvesant finally decided on an all-out war with New Sweden to permanently secure the region for the Dutch. Shortly after the fall of Fort Casimir, the governor ordered a much-anticipated Swedish supply ship docking at New Amsterdam on its way to Delaware to be seized. The *Gyllene Haj* (*Golden Shark*) was held by Dutch authorities, its crew imprisoned and its cargo sold off. Five of the ship's compliment managed to eventually reach Fort Christina with a message: the Swedes were to abandon their colonies or face conquest. When combined with the fact that the recent war between the Dutch and English had just ended, the Swedes were justifiably concerned. Governor Rising responded by reinforcing Christina with most of the men and equipment from Fort Trinity, including 150 pounds of gunpowder, muskets, swords and pikes.

By the end of August 1655, the Dutch sailed up the Delaware with seven warships and 317 men. Aboard the *Wagh*, a thirty-two gun ship (which was the largest vessel in New Netherlands), Stuyvesant approached Fort Christina with more men than existed in the Swedish colony at the time. Along the way from New Amsterdam, his armada had stopped at Sandy Hook to take prisoners and interrogate the local Dutch. Now he sailed "amidst the beating of drums and blowing of trumpets and a great bravado," past Fort Trinity, landing his men at

Strand Point.[21] The Swedish commander at the post, Sven Schute, allowed Stuyvesant to pass without even firing a shot, an action for which he would later be court-martialed. Having cut off Fort Trinity from Fort Christina, Stuyvesant sent an emissary to demand the commander's surrender while his troops began to entrench around the Swedish position. Though they were promised that they could evacuate the fort "with flying banners, full arms, burning fuses, bullet in your mouth and more similar things," Schute refused.[22] Yet the small size of his force, combined with riots and mutinies that erupted among his men, compelled Schute to fall to his knees before Stuyvesant and beg pardon.

The Dutch next approached Fort Christina and began a bombardment of the capital of New Sweden by the first week of September. On that same day, Printzhoff, the old manor home of Governor Printz, was pillaged, and the village of Christineham was burned to the ground. The capital held out for almost two weeks before finally surrendering to the Dutch army on September 18. New Sweden had fallen after only seventeen years of existence, leaving little permanent impact on the region (save for proving the desirability of settling the Delaware region and showing that the river was not a northwest passage to China).

Peach Tree War

Yet the Dutch settlements in New Jersey were hardly at peace following the expulsion of the Swedes. In fact, the assault by Stuyvesant on New Sweden led directly to another bloody conflict on the soil of New Jersey. On September 15, 1655, while the vast majority of the soldiers of New Amsterdam were finishing up their siege of Fort Christina, an armada of sixty-four war canoes approached Manhattan. Over five hundred Susquehannock landed south of Wall Street and began to fan out across the city. Though nominally allied with the Swedes, the natives told the inhabitants of the island that they were simply passing through on their way to attack other tribes on Long Island. Remaining in the town all day, the Indians became more of a nuisance, forcing their way into various Dutch homes, stealing possessions and fighting citizens. In fact, at the time, the Dutch blamed the killing of a native girl who had stolen a peach for the assault itself.

By nightfall, as tensions mounted, Cornelis van Tienhoven ordered the men at the fort to attack the natives. After the shooting began, three Indians and two colonists were killed. In response, the Susquehannock proceeded to assault and burn Pavonia, Hoboken and Communipaw in New Jersey, all of which could be seen aflame from Manhattan by morning. The majority of the settlers in those areas were quickly killed or captured, with 150 prisoners being held at Paulus Hook alone. Approximately one thousand more natives quickly arrived in the region, with the assault soon spreading to Staten Island. By the time the war died out a few days later, fifty Dutch colonists had been killed, over one hundred women and children abducted, twenty-eight boweries burned and five to six hundred cattle destroyed. At the same time the Dutch were clearing the Swedish from the Delaware and southern New Jersey, the Peach Tree War weakened their hold on the northeastern part of the state. A further conflict between the two groups that lasted from 1659 to 1663, known as the Esopus War, drove more tribes of native refugees into the area of northern New Jersey to seek shelter with the Ramapo.

ANGLO-DUTCH WAR

As the Dutch consolidated their power on both the Delaware and the Hudson Rivers, the English were becoming concerned at this growing colonial wedge that was driven between Virginia and Massachusetts Bay. The Dutch, for their part, were in no rush to colonize New Jersey but did begin the process of re-fortifying their boweries in Bergen County. In 1660, a palisaded fort was duly constructed at Bergen Square in present-day Jersey City. Three years later, the Crown granted the Duke of York a charter to all of the lands in present-day New York, New Jersey and Connecticut. Wasting little time, a small fleet was fitted out in Portsmouth, England, carrying three companies of men and escorted by four frigates, including the *Guinea*, a fourth-rate ship carrying thirty-eight cannon. Richard Nicolls led the flotilla into New York Harbor after picking up additional men off Coney Island. Yet these reinforcements proved to be unneeded as a lack of arms, discontent at the company's handling of the constant Indian incursions and the absence of Stuyvesant led New Amsterdam to surrender unconditionally on August 29, 1664. By September 24, George Cartwright had captured Fort Orange at present-day Albany, and shortly after, the Delaware region surrendered to Sir Richard Carr. In a quick, decisive strike, England had united its northern and southern colonies. New Jersey was firmly in English hands.

CHAPTER 2

NEW JERSEY IN THE WARS OF EMPIRE: COLONIAL NEW JERSEY'S MILITARY HISTORY

The Duke of York soon divided the territory of New Jersey between John Berkeley, the Baron of Stratton, and Sir George Carteret. In fact, the territory owes its very name to Carteret's defense of its namesake Channel Island in 1649 against the forces of Parliament. Many of the initial settlers were likewise former soldiers of fortune, both Cavaliers and Roundheads who were either granted lands as rewards or who sought a fresh start in the New World. The dangers still prevalent in the region were well understood as settlers were granted 150 acres, provided they had "a good musket, bandoliers, and match convenient."[23] War followed the men of England to New Jersey as both Native American tribes and European powers sought to challenge their claim to the region.

King Philip's War

The outbreak of King Philip's War in New England in 1675 would test the military readiness of the new colony. Though no major battles took place in the state, the sheer number of natives within its borders and the early victories of King Philip spread panic through the ranks of the settlers. As early as the summer of 1673, the town council of Newark had ordered all men between the ages of sixteen and sixty to appear on the morning of October 1 with a gun, a half pound of powder and twelve bullets. Evidently satisfied with their military readiness, the settlement next set about establishing a fortified defensive position. In 1675, the town ordered the meetinghouse to be fortified against possible attack. The lower half was barricaded with stone and mortar, while additional strongpoints were constructed at two corners of the church. On September 10, the town council asked overseers of the project to report anyone slacking in their duties during construction. At the same time, a resident of the town, John Ward, was tasked with acquiring ample supplies of powder and lead for bullets. The possibility of an Indian assault was being taken very seriously.

Other parts of the colony reacted in a similar way. In 1673, Piscataway raised a regiment under Captain Francis Drake, which some historians argue to be the earliest predecessor to the famed Jersey Blues. Their uniform consisted of a deerskin conical hat, a dark blue shirt and pants to the knees with four buttons, allegedly one button each for Piscataway, Perth Amboy, Woodbridge and Bridgeton.[24] Town records from Woodbridge state that the regiment was raised to "control Indians who came down from western New York and upper Pennsylvania in the summers, to gorge themselves on fishes and clambs [sic] and make a general nuisance of themselves. They become drunk and burn haystack."[25] On June 10, 1670, Newark would organize its first effective town watch to patrol the streets at night. Three men would serve in shifts, ready to raise the alarm in case of attack. Additionally, the town mandated that all male citizens would drill on Sundays, a quarter of them each week to prepare for duty.[26]

The war itself would never reach the colony of New Jersey. Yet some intrepid men did venture north to aid their fellow colonists in battling for survival. One of the most famous was Robert Treat, the founder of Newark, who returned to Connecticut in 1672 and commanded the militia in their war with the natives.

THE THIRD ANGLO-DUTCH WAR

In 1672, England and the Netherlands entered into yet another war with each other. As with many of the other conflicts of the era, it quickly became a world war. In August 1673, a Dutch fleet appeared off Staten

Island. It had been only eight years since New Netherlands had fallen to Richard Nichols, and they were anything but securely in English hands. On August 8, six hundred Dutch soldiers landed above Wall Street and marched on Fort James. Captain Manning, the English commander at the post, had fewer than sixty men at his disposal. In addition, in an ironic repeat of history, Governor Francis Lovelace was absent from the colony, much as Stuyvesant had been during its fall to the English a decade prior. New York quickly surrendered and was renamed New Orange by Director General Anthony Colve.

New Jersey had been in periodic rebellion ever since its establishment, and the arrival of the Dutch was seen by many to be a welcomed invasion. The policies of Berkeley and Carteret had provoked determined resistance on the part of recent arrivals and landowners. As early as June 1667, a local assembly in the Highlands was talking of seeking independence. In 1668, deputies from the towns of Middletown and Shrewsbury refused to take oaths to the colonial assembly, while residents of the town refused to pay taxes or publish colonial ordinances. Finally, in May 1672, representatives from Elizabethtown, Newark, Woodbridge, Piscataway and Bergen had gathered and elected James Carteret as "president of the country." In fact, a resident of Elizabethtown by the name of Samuel Hopkins had, after being captured by the invasion fleet, assured them that "New Yorke was in no condicon to defend itself against the Dutch, but they had few canons mounted and those that were upon such rotten cariages that one discharge would shake them to peeces."[27]

Representatives of Elizabethtown, Newark, Woodbridge and Piscataway did all dutifully appear before the Dutch authorities to surrender following the fall of New York City. Bergen, Middletown and Shrewsbury were all threatened to likewise submit or face attack. Director General Colve reinstituted Dutch rule throughout the region, which became known again as AchterColl, or "Back of the Bay."

Yet the war in Europe was drawing to a close, and foreign policy, not force of arms, would determine the future of New Jersey. On February 9, 1674, England and the Netherlands signed the Treaty of Westminster, ending hostilities between the two nations. As part of the peace agreement, New York and New Jersey were returned to the English Crown in exchange for more valuable colonies elsewhere.

CARTERET'S WAR

The Dutch episode had scarcely come to an end in New Jersey when another foreign invasion threatened its shores. Though anger over the rule of Philip Carteret had divided the young colony, it soon united in response to this new challenge. Yet far from being a distant enemy the newest belligerent arrived from just over the Hudson River.

The confusing nature of patents granted by the Crown in the seventeenth century led to a territorial dispute between Carteret and the recently appointed governor of New York, Edmund Andros. Though more well known to Americans for his rule over the despised Dominion of New England, Andros first became involved in America farther south in the Middle Colonies. Claiming East Jersey as part of his bailiwick, Andros wrote to Carteret on March 8, 1679, demanding that the latter and his officials immediately remove themselves from office. Philip Carteret had been appointed by his cousin George Carteret as governor in 1665 and felt secure in his claim to power. This is clearly shown in a letter that Carteret wrote in reply to Andros on March 20: "If any force be used to defend ourselves and our families the best we can, which is any blood be shed, it will be contrary to our desires, and the just and righteous God require it at your Hands, who are the Causes thereof…an alarm we had yesterday of your being come with your sloops and a considerable number of soldiers which constrained us to put ourselves in a posture of defense."[28] As war with New York seemed inevitable, Newark voted to arm on March 22. A system was also established by the town's assembly to relay an alarm through the village consisting of a "drum from Joseph Riggs' gate and Sam. Harrison's gate and three shots to be signal."

On April 7, Andros and a band of armed followers landed at Elizabethtown. Governor Carteret raised 150 men in arms to greet the neighboring governor, no doubt hoping this show of force would dissuade any offensive action on the part of Andros. The residents of the provincial capital likewise gathered up weapons and ammunition to protect themselves and their property. Yet the initial meeting proved to be a peaceful affair, with each side presenting its arguments over a pleasant dinner and with Carteret accompanying Andros to his sloop at the end of the night.

However, the governor of New York, upon returning to his capital, issued a warrant for the arrest of Carteret, citing how he had "with Force

Sir Edmund Andros after his arrest. *From William A. Crafts's* Pioneers in the Settlement of America, *Vol. 1 (1876).*

and Arms, riotously and routonsly with Capt. John Berry, Capt. William Sanford, and several other person, hath presumed to exercise jurisdiction and government over his majesty's subjects."[29] Rather than seek to battle the militia of New Jersey, Andros decided on a quick assault on the home of Carteret under the cover of darkness. Therefore, on the night of April 30, the governor of New Jersey was seized from his bed "as naked as he was" and quickly carried off to New York City. In the words of Carteret himself, "he sent a Party of Soldiers to fetch me away Dead or alive, so that in the Dead Time of the Night broke open my Doors and most barbarously and inhumanly and violently hailed me out of my Bed, that I have not Words enough sufficiently to express the Cruelty of it; and Indeed I am so disabled by the Bruises and Hurts I then received, that I fear I shall hardly be a perfect Man again."[30]

The governor of New Jersey would be held in a New York prison for over a month. He was eventually put on trial, yet in the end, a jury would acquit him of the charges brought against him by Andros. Though reinstated by the Duke of York, the brutality of his seizure would lead to his death only six months later. The brief war between New York and New Jersey produced only loss for Andros and death for Carteret.

GLORIOUS REVOLUTION

The Glorious (or Bloodless) Revolution was welcomed both in England and in many parts of the American colonies. Nowhere is this more evident than in the history of New Jersey during that time period. The autocratic rule of the Stuarts combined with fears of a Popish plot to affect various instances of rebellion and regicide in England. One of these, the Rye House Plot of 1683, which centered on the killing of the king and his son, bore direct and indirect relations to New Jersey. One of the main conspirators, Robert West, owned shares in East Jersey. In addition, of the four original counties in the colony, one was named for the Duke of Monmouth, the illegitimate son of Charles II who had been banished in 1679 for his involvement in a movement to exclude James from the throne. Monmouth was subsequently implicated in the Rye House Plot as well and was this time exiled in 1684 to the Netherlands. Naming a county in a colony after such an individual was not a harmless act.

Following the death of Charles and the ascension of his son as James II, further revolts erupted across England. Monmouth himself returned to the island nation to lead an uprising against the Catholic sovereign. In the end, this attempt resulted in only failure and the execution of the duke. Hundreds of Covenanters, Whigs and personal enemies of James II were condemned to Barbados and America. At least one shipload of

The Duke of Monmouth. *National Portrait Gallery of London.*

exiles arrived in Perth Amboy, New Jersey, on December 7, 1685, aboard the *Henry and Francis*. A few years later, in 1688, the colony named its newest county Somerset, after the location of the Bloody Assizes, the trials by which James II punished those who had rebelled against him.

The English monarch began to respond to such provocative moves by the colony in 1688. The colonial capital of Perth Amboy lost its overseas trading privileges, a devastating blow to the province's economy. As well, Governor Andros was finally granted direct rule over the entire region, ending a decade-long struggle for power. Yet in the end, these moves proved to be short-lived, as William of Orange landed in England and deposed James II by the end of the year.

Repercussions from the Glorious Revolution continued to reverberate through New Jersey for years after the event. Andrew Hamilton, who had been colonial governor of the colony from 1692 to 1697, had been deposed by Parliament due to his Scottish birth. During his tenure, he had annually experienced difficulties from the Quaker members of the assembly, especially with regards to funding for operations against natives and the French during King William's War. Yet the misadministration of his successor brought Hamilton back into power in 1699.

Not only the governor's return but also his subsequent appointments began to anger many of the residents of New Jersey. In Monmouth County alone, the newly appointed sheriff and clerk were both Scottish. Residents of the region began to again raise the charge that a non-Englishman could not rule over them. Complaints and rumors began to spread:

> For was it not proved by the written declarations of three honest Quakers of Shrewsbury township, that Lewis Morris had said openly in their presence at the house of Abraham Brown in that township, that he had taken an office from Governor Hamilton, and would enforce his authority or "spill the blood of any man who resisted him" [and] that he "would go through with his office though the streets run with blood."[31]

Fears and anger over the rule of Hamilton finally came to a head in March 1700. A group of men in Monmouth County called to be jurors at the first sitting of the new court challenged the legitimacy of the court officers. When summoned, the old clerk even refused to hand over the previous session's records unless he received a promissory note protecting him in case of a subsequent lawsuit over his doing so. Indignant over these responses, the officials had the men seized and held in contempt. Yet after a two-hour recess, all of the citizens were released, being instead subjected to fines. This change of heart was reported to have been the product of fear on the part of the judges as they were in "the enemy's camp."[32]

Attempts by the sheriff to collect these fines on July 17, 1700, resulted in his being assaulted by a group of local men. That same month, the arrival of Governor Hamilton and council president Lewis Morris, accompanied by fifty armed men, was likewise confronted by one hundred militiamen of Middletown, though no violence erupted. Yet residents of the county finally decided to take decisive action at the next sitting of the court in the spring of 1701. In March of that year, a fake pirate was brought to the court by local residents. Citizens alleged that he had sailed with Captain Kidd and demanded a trial. During the proceedings, a local innkeeper named Samuel Willett suddenly stood up and exclaimed that the "governor and justice had no authority to hold court, and should break it up."[33] Another resident arose and began to beat a drum, at which point thirty to forty armed militiamen charged the floor of the courthouse. The sheriff, after attempting to hold them back, was severely beaten, at which time the justices and the king's attorney drew their swords and leapt into the fray. However, numbers were on the side of the townspeople. By the end of the fight, Governor Hamilton, the sheriff, the justices, the king's attorney and the clerk had all been captured.

The men would be held from March 25 to March 29, and though they were eventually released relatively unharmed, a clear message had been delivered. As town leaders had purposefully scheduled the training of the militia for the same day, the revolt was an organized affair. Morris soon sailed to England to raise forces to punish the rebellious residents of New Jersey. Yet before any further action could be taken, Governor Hamilton was removed from office and appointed deputy governor of Pennsylvania by William Penn. East and West Jersey were subsequently combined into one royal colony by Queen Anne. To further reduce the often-violent independence of the colonists, both New York and New Jersey would, in fact, share a governor from 1702 to 1738. Unfortunately, the first such appointment, a moral rake and alleged cross-dresser, did little to endear colonists to the Crown. A revolution that began as an attack on the centralizing and autocratic rule of the Stuarts ended in more autocratic and centralized rule being brought to the colonies.

QUEEN ANNE'S WAR

In the midst of the reorganization of New Jersey as a royal colony, another global, colonial war erupted between Great Britain and France. Yet a series of combative royal governors, recent hostilities between the colony and its mother country and a powerful and pacifist block of Quakers within the assembly would all challenge New Jersey's participation in the conflict. Despite these misgivings, New Jersey's coastal position placed it early on within the theater of war. French privateers began to ply the heavily trafficked waters off the Jersey shore. As the lifeline of the British economy was the trade ships that sailed up the American coast from Jamaica on their way to England, the undefended shoreline of New Jersey proved to be an ideal hunting ground for intrepid French warships.

In one infamous episode, a French privateer plundered ships for weeks along the Jersey shore. In early June 1704, an English merchantman sailing from Antigua was seized by a French warship of fourteen guns under the command of Captain Davy in the Delaware Bay. Davy then proceeded up the Jersey shore, chasing another ship toward Sandy Hook. When no further prizes were found, the French instead landed twenty-four men below the Navesink River and proceeded to burn two homes to the ground. The incident threatened to place not only the shipping off New Jersey but also its coastal settlements on the front line of Queen Anne's War. Residents of the county established a watch system that was tasked with preventing further raids. Yet the assaults on shipping continued.

On June 27, the French privateer engaged another English vessel that had sailed to America from London. The merchantman attempted to avoid capture by beaching itself on Sandy Hook. However, when this maneuver failed, the captain and his crew, including Philip French, the former mayor of New York City, abandoned the ship and fled. They rowed to the Jersey shore and were rescued by the local militia.

Anger and frustration over the raids, combined with the apparent lack of English action, led the citizens of the region to fit out their own privateers. A Dutch ship docked in New York City under the command of Adrian Claver was hired on July 27 to pursue the French ship. Two days later, additional Jersey ships were fitted out under Captains Evertson and Penniston. Shortly afterward, they were joined by the British warship

HMS *Jersey*, and all four patrolled the waters off the coast of Staten Island. Between July 31 and August 7, two additional English merchantmen were taken, and yet no progress was made in stopping the ravages of Captain Davy.

Governor Cornbury called the assembly together in September 1704 to request funds for the construction of a watchtower on the Atlantic Highlands with enough militia to patrol the area. Despite weeks of debate, the bill was delayed, and the Jersey shore continued to be a theater of war. The next summer, another French privateer, perhaps Davy, again raided the waters off Sandy Hook, capturing a ship bound for Jamaica. A French raiding party again landed south of the Navesink and burned more homes to the ground. Four American boats loaded with 350 men were again dispatched to clear the region, though much as in 1704, they failed to encounter the nimble Frenchman. A few months of peace passed until October, when two more ships bound for Jamaica were seized. The English trade route to Jamaica was being slowly strangled. Finally moved to action, signal towers were constructed at Sandy Hook and the Atlantic Highlands, each manned by a three-man contingent and equipped with loud cannons to warn the residents of New York City.

Under this atmosphere of constant attack and raids, Governor Cornbury again called the assembly together in 1707 to urge the raising of troops and commitment of money. Speaker Samuel Jennings, a Quaker, led his sizeable minority to oppose the governor's plan. Jennings and Lewis Morris, now an assemblyman, even began to petition the queen to remove the corrupt and alleged cross-dressing Cornbury. Anne finally relented in December 1708, removing the governor and replacing him with a series of short-lived individuals.

Most notable among these was Richard Ingoldesby, who became acting governor in May 1709. The "Glorious Enterprise," a joint land-sea invasion of Canada, was then being planned in both England and the American colonies. Based on a previous failed invasion strategy from 1690, the plan called for American and Native American troops to march up the Hudson while English forces proceeded down the St. Lawrence. New Jersey's quota of two hundred men was heavily opposed by the Quaker minority in the assembly. A compromise bill calling for £3,000 to fund two hundred "volunteers" was eventually proposed. Though the Quakers would still vote against the bill, they knew that enough votes existed to pass the measure and thus spare New Jersey the ignominy of appearing to be disloyal to the Crown. Yet it was at this moment that Ingoldesby decided to move against the Society of Friends. The governor had a few of his key allies change their votes, thus dooming the bill. Following its defeat, he then prorogued the assembly and awaited the results of the invasion, which would have discredited his enemies in the legislature regardless of whether it succeeded.

Ultimately, Generals Nicholson and Vetch, the leaders of the expedition, convinced Ingoldesby to recall the assembly after only ten days and vote the necessary measures through. The funds granted for the volunteers represented the first-ever printing of paper currency in the colony of New Jersey. Yet despite all the drama associated with the passing of the bill, the invasion force failed to acquire the necessary British backing and dissolved after weeks of inaction at Albany. In the end, the only casualty of the "Glorious Enterprise" was Ingoldesby himself. Recalled in late 1709, he was replaced the next year by Robert Hunter, a veteran of the war who had fought with Marlborough at Blenheim and Ramillies and had been held captive by the French from 1707 to 1709.

In fact, the Quaker-filled assembly of New Jersey kept the colony out of most of the major battles of the war, including the famed conquest of Port Royal in 1710. The one major expedition to which New Jersey eventually committed was a repeat of the "Glorious Enterprise," the Quebec Expedition of 1711. Much as in previous attempts, a two-pronged invasion of Canada by land and sea was to be undertaken in the hopes of capturing Quebec. In August 1711, General Nicholson departed from Albany with four thousand men, including troops from New Jersey, New York and Connecticut. Unfortunately for the colonials, the British fleet that had sailed down the St. Lawrence to support the invasion wrecked, leading to the loss of over eight hundred lives. When news of the disaster reached Nicholson at Lake George, he abandoned his expedition. New Jersey's participation in Queen Anne's War produced little for the state. Dozens of English merchantmen were captured or sunk, the colony's contribution of troops accomplished nothing of value and the deep divisions within its ruling structure were laid bare.

War of Jenkins' Ear (1739–48)

In 1739, war erupted between Great Britain and Spain, ostensibly over the mutilation of an English merchant captain. Once again, the conflict became a worldwide affair fought on multiple continents. The English would specifically focus their attention on the Spanish possessions in the Caribbean, and it was into these resource-rich areas that New Jersey sent its first soldiers abroad.

Once again, the colony's coastal location quickly invited attacks by privateers. Spanish warships soon appeared off Sandy Hook and in the Delaware Bay. In May 1740 alone, three Spanish ships began to seize prizes off the coast. In response, the assembly approved £400 to fund the hiring of two privateers to hunt down the Spanish. Later that same year, Governor Morris convinced the assembly of the need to raise three one-hundred-man regiments. Yet unlike in Queen Anne's War, these provincial troops were to be sent much farther than the frontier of New York.

In October 1740, the raised New Jersey troops departed from both Perth Amboy and down the Delaware River. The soldiers sailed along the Atlantic coast, arriving at Jamaica in January 1741 to join up with other colonial troops as well as British regulars. While on the island, the men were engaged in helping to suppress the remnants of a slave rebellion known as the Maroon Revolt. This massive uprising, which had raged on and off for decades, was occurring at the same time as the New York Slave Conspiracy of 1741 and suspected slave uprisings in Hackensack and other parts of New Jersey.

The American units under the command of Colonel William Gooch, the governor of Virginia, landed in Jamaica before their British counterparts. They quickly discovered that while supplies were lacking, disease was rampant. Casualties among the colonials, unused to the tropical diseases of the Caribbean, soon began to mount, crippling the regiments before battle was even joined. Upon the eventual arrival of the English, the American units were attached to the expedition of Admiral Edward Vernon, and the thirty-thousand-man force sailed in over 180 vessels to its objective of Cartagena de Indias in modern-day Colombia.

The target of the English assault was one of the most important Spanish settlements in the Americas, as it controlled the flow of silver and other treasures from South America to Cuba and onward to Spain. While the Spanish mounted over three hundred cannon to defend the city, they would depend on a far more devious weapon with which to protect themselves. Admiral Blas de Lezo relied on a delaying tactic, holding off the English assault until the rainy season. It was his hope that the yellow fever that normally arose in those months would devastate the British army in a far more effective way than the musket fire of his men.

After a little over two months, Vernon ended his assault. Over 18,000 of his men were dead or incapacitated, almost all of them from yellow fever or dysentery. Only about 10 percent of the 3,700 Americans returned home as well. Included in this number was Lawrence Washington, the brother of our first president, who would go on to name his newly acquired home Mount Vernon after his commander. The first use of both American and New Jersey troops abroad had ended in dismal failure.

KING GEORGE'S WAR (1744–48)

As the War of Jenkins' Ear raged on, the British once again found themselves at war with the French. Although the causes of the war lay in a struggle for succession to the crown of Austria, to the American colonists, it simply meant another "Glorious Enterprise" into Canada. For New Jersey specifically, it meant dangers to shipping, the fear of coastal invasion and the demands of the Crown to participate in foreign adventurism.

Governor William Shirley of Massachusetts, fearful of his own colony's coastal weakness, organized an expedition to attack the French fortress at Louisbourg. Shirley's letters and pleas helped to piece together a force of over four thousand men, transports and privateers. All of New England, New York and even the Quaker-dominated assemblies of Pennsylvania and New Jersey pledged men, money and equipment. New Jersey itself sent five hundred men and £2,000, half of which was in produce from the farms of the Garden State. Joined by a British squadron under Admiral William Pepperell, the task force arrived off the coast of Nova Scotia in May 1745. For over a month, the English and Americans attacked the fortress of Louisbourg, before the town and its defensive works finally surrendered on June 28.

At the same time that troops from New Jersey were assaulting the defensive works on Cape Breton Island, the colony's shores were being attacked by both French and Spanish ships. In July 1747, Spanish privateers landed at Taylor's Bridge, Delaware, across the river from Lower Alloway Creek, raiding a series of homes and kidnapping slaves and servants. Across the Delaware, the New Jersey Assembly pledged money, much as in the previous war, to fund local ships to combat privateers. At the height of the conflict, the signal beacon that had been constructed atop the Atlantic Highlands during Queen Anne's War accidently burned to the ground. Despite the design of the structure to warn New York City of approaching privateers by signal fire, no one on the island of Manhattan reportedly noticed the burning tower, perhaps a testament to its uselessness. Sea fights would continue off the Jersey shore even after the formal declaration of peace in April 1748. On June 4 of that year, nearly a month and a half after the signing of a truce and the opening of the peace conference at Aix-la-Chapelle, Captain John Burgess of the *Royal Catherine* fought and captured the French vessel *Le Mars* after an engagement off Sandy Hook.

Additional troops from New Jersey and Great Britain would also be raised to help defend the coastline of the colony and its capital as well. Various units were housed during the war at Parker Castle in Perth Amboy. Razed in 1942, this imposing structure was built by the Parker family around the turn of the eighteenth century. Commanding the heights between Front and Water Streets on the Arthur Kill Sound, the building would serve as a fortress to protect the capital of the province during the war.

In 1746, word began to circulate among the northern colonies that the British were again to attempt a Glorious Enterprise into Canada. Much as in previous wars, this invasion would operate on two axes: a naval expedition down the St. Lawrence and an overland invasion up the Hudson. The assembly of New Jersey pledged 500 men in June 1746. Excitement regarding the proposed invasion can be seen from the fact that, in the end, over 660 men would sign up, far surpassing the colony's quota. Five companies were organized, and in September, these soldiers slowly made their way from Perth Amboy to Albany, where they joined growing army being assembled there.

Unfortunately, much as in their arrival at Jamaica five years before, the men found few supplies and none of the promised English reinforcements. Provisions quickly ran out, and anger erupted among the soldiers. The

A photograph of Parker Castle in Perth Amboy during the late 1800s.
Author's collection.

commissioners of the New Jersey units were particularly targeted for
their lack of foresight. Young Colonel Peter Schuyler, who would later go
on to achieve fame in the French and Indian War, personally appealed
to the legislature over issues of missing supplies and a lack of pay. Even
though Governor Belcher ordered immediate relief, the assembly failed
to act. Schuyler himself was required to suppress the near mutiny among
the men, personally handing out money to cover the needs of the now
forgotten army.

The Treaty of Aix-la-Chapelle ended the war in 1748. Rather
than a glorious victory, the English and French had largely reached a
stalemate. In the end, various colonies and islands were traded between
the world superpowers, with more being achieved at the peace table
than on the battlefield. The New Jersey troops at Albany returned home,
accomplishing nothing and having lost men to disease, starvation and

desertion. Most infuriating to the colonies in general was the return of Louisbourg to the French. The great expedition organized by Shirley, and the loss of life by New Jersey and the other colonies, was seen by many Americans to have been all for naught.

New Jersey Land Riots

While England waged its wars for empire, the colonists of New Jersey were again rising up against their own government. The confusing nature of the initial colonization of the province led to disputes over land ownership. For three quarters of a century, multiple individuals had granted the same tracks of land to different people. A man's status as a "freeman" was connected to his land ownership; thus, failure to show proper documentation could lead to a potential loss of civil rights. A cycle of violence, arrest, mob justice and rebellion soon flared up across New Jersey and continued for over a decade.

In early September 1745, Samuel Baldwin was arrested for trespassing while chopping wood on his own land, part of the Horseneck Track in West Essex. His warrant read, "Baldwin made great havock [sic] with his said saw mills of the best timber…to the great improverishment of the land."[34] He was transported to the Broad Street Jail in Newark to stand trial, refusing the offers of his neighbors to pay his bail. Then, on September 19, a mob of 150 men led by Timothy Meeker and armed with axes, clubs and other improvised weapons freed Baldwin. Members of the group informed the authorities that if another resident were arrested, they would return not only in force but with Indians as well.

A Newark freeholder by the name of Amos Roberts soon became the leader of the movement. Though a landowner, his family had migrated from New England, and he was thus viewed as an outsider by the town's elites. Roberts began to gather more disaffected men about him, holding meetings at various taverns across East Jersey. The first test of Roberts's movement came in January 1746. On the fifteenth of that month, Robert Young, Thomas Sergeant and Nehemiah Baldwin were arrested for their actions during the previous riot in Newark. Hoping to avert a similar situation as had occurred the previous fall, the sheriff of Essex County called out the militia. Perhaps showing where the loyalties of the townspeople lay, or simply out of fear, only fifteen militiamen responded to the sheriff's call. Worse yet, when these men were ordered to remove the three prisoners to the judge, only six agreed to do so.

The next morning, one of the prisoners, Nehemiah Baldwin, asked to be taken before the judge to pay his bail. While the sheriff was escorting him there, a mob armed with clubs appeared and violently freed Baldwin. The sheriff retreated back to the jail, again calling up the militia; twenty-six would answer his summons and arrive to help him guard the building. As the sheriff and his men escorted the remaining two prisoners from the jail at two o'clock in the afternoon, they were confronted by an augmented mob. Three hundred men under the command of Amos Roberts blocked the streets in front of the sheriff. Though two judges appeared and read the riot act, Roberts's men did not disperse. At the same time, the sheriff's attempt to use two drummers to gather more militia failed as well. Roberts than called out, "Those who are upon my list, follow me."[35] His men charged the sheriff, and his militia, through shear violence, freed the remaining two prisoners.

According to the rioters, though, no one was "dangerously wounded." Governor Morris immediately appeared before the assembly and on March 4 issued a formal complaint requesting that the legislature act to put down the revolt. The assembly responded by having a militia bill prepared. In April, the rioters themselves also addressed the government, sending two letters to Perth Amboy outlining their arguments and demands. In response, though that same month the council passed an "Act for Preventing Tumults and Riotous Assemblies" that limited all public meetings over twelve people, the assembly tabled the measure, refusing to pass it until the law had been printed and publicly distributed.

On August 5, 1746, yet another riot broke out, this time in Bergen County. Forty men armed with clubs proceeded to the two-hundred-acre property of Edward Jeffers. He had been in disputes with various farmers over ownership of the land. The threats of the rioters convinced Jeffers to back down and hand over half of his land, providing another victory for the anti-proprietary party. Perhaps the most unique aspect of this episode was the identity of the mob's leader, a widow named Magdalena Valleau. The situation was repeated a month later in Essex County when groups of rioters from Newark broke up the property of John Burnet, which consisted of almost two thousand acres.

Further riots would continue for the next few years across the state. In December 1746, a mob from Newark began to plan a march on the colonial capital, stating that its goal was to "level Perth Amboy to the ground" and push English governance "into the sea." Though the expected riot never materialized, talk of it rattled legislators and citizens in the capital. The next year, a jailbreak of debtors did take place in Somerset County, while another mob from Essex again threatened to march on Perth Amboy, this time targeting the home of Assemblyman Samuel Nevill. On March 20, 1747, a group of thirty armed men attacked the home of Joseph Dalrymple on the Passaic River in Morris County. The door was ripped off Dalrymple's house as they attempted to remove him by force from his estate. Yet thanks to the presence of his pregnant wife and one-year-old child, the mob "graciously" gave him fourteen days to vacate the property. An attempt a month later on the home of Justice Daniel Coopers was averted only due to the presence of one hundred armed officers.

By 1747, Amos Roberts had basically established himself as the ruler of an independent state. He organized a mob in July of that year to free thirty prisoners from the prison in Perth Amboy who were being held for levying war against the king. Roberts set up wards within the city, appointed officials to organize the people, dispatched tax collectors, established courts and organized and trained a militia. Though the assembly was not on the side of the rioters, it provided little resistance to Roberts, instead preferring to place the blame at the feet of the governor and his council for not enforcing the laws already on the books.

Protests and revolts only grew larger over the next few years. Taverns were crowded with plotting mobs, estates and homes were seized, workers absconded with livestock or property and massive bonfire rallies became a common sight. In 1749 alone, newspapers reported that a large group of Horseneck rioters fired off guns into the air and danced all night around a large fire to celebrate the expulsion of an upper-class tenant.

Yet a mob dedicated to anarchic redistribution is not a stable structure. The power of Roberts and others like him proved to be only temporary. More and more farmers and workers who made up the riotous groups began to drift away as economic and familial concerns trumped the idealism of leveling. In September 1752, Roberts himself was arrested and held for a few days before he was finally broken out, an unthinkable

The location of various land riots in New Jersey in the 1740s. *Author's collection.*

situation only a few years before. Fewer than ten followers came to the prison in disguises well after dark before they attempted the feat. A similar situation unfolded with Simon Wyckoff of the Harrison Tract that same year. Though violence continued sporadically in New Jersey well into the 1790s, especially in the Ramapo region, the concerns of the colony and its residents soon turned to more pressing military matters. Yet the actions of the colonists for the rights of landowners proved to be a precursor for the actions of the next, Revolutionary generation.

FRENCH AND INDIAN WAR (1754–63)

When conflict next erupted between the French and the English, it represented the most deadly threat yet to the colony of New Jersey. The French and Indian War would decide the dominant power in North America, and its battles would be fought in almost every possession of the two colonial powers. With its open and well-traveled coastline, its proximity to the Canadian border and the presence of large groups of Native Americans, New Jersey almost immediately felt the effects of the conflict.

The New Jersey Assembly followed the lead of other colonial legislatures by immediately declaring loyalty to the British Crown. Yet at the same time, lawmakers in Perth Amboy informed the governor that they had no money with which to pursue the conflict. Governor Belcher himself stated that this move was "unusual if not without precedent."[36] Subsequent requests by the Crown for New Jersey to contribute £500 and 120 men were met with conditional promises, hinged upon Governor Belcher's approval of a loan bill. When the governor refused their demand, instead proposing a tax, the assembly adjourned. Calls from Virginia for aid were subsequently ignored, and the state likewise refused to send representatives to Benjamin Franklin's Albany Congress, which had been called to organize the colonies for their common defense.

Yet the state did slowly awaken to the dangers of war. The new assembly was warned by the governor of French encroachments when it first sat in October 1754. Three months later, on New Year's Day, Aaron Burr Sr., the president of the College of New Jersey (later Princeton University), likewise delivered an address concerning the threat presented by the French and their Indian allies in which he called for "immediate, united and vigorous measures for repelling the insults of our enemies and defending our country and liberties."[37]

Various pieces of legislation began to emerge from the assembly house, slowly placing New Jersey on war footing. A law was passed to pardon all rioters, slowly moving the colony away from the land disputes that had crippled it for a decade. In March 1755, £500 was raised to help transport English troops across the state as they moved toward the Ohio region. At the same time, vessels from the state were prohibited from trading with the French.

Yet the assembly still hesitated to raise actual soldiers. Governor Belcher was informed that existing militia laws were adequate and that these men would only be raised and dispatched should the frontiers of New York be breached. Peter Schuyler, disheartened by this news, volunteered to raise four hundred men with his own money to march to the defense of New York City. In response, Governor Belcher proposed the raising of five hundred men on April 24, 1755, under Schuyler. The assembly approved of the measure, but rather than employing conscription, it instead promised thirty-shilling bounties. Citizens of the colony proved to be more eager than their legislature to support the war effort, and by May, four of the five companies had already been formed. A letter from the time period relates how "every body is willing to contribute a Mite against the French and the Country Fellows list like mad."[38] Captain Nathaniel Rusco alone filled his company in less than eleven days.

The threat to New Jersey began to become clearer and more pressing as the year progressed. Governor Belcher called the assembly together in July to inform them of Braddock's disastrous defeat in Pennsylvania. A month later, refugees from Native raids in Pennsylvania began to trickle into western New Jersey, bringing with them tales of horror and massacre. Perhaps the most pressing moment for the colony came with the Gnadenhutten Massacre on November 24, 1755.

News of this atrocity prompted the militia from Sussex and Morris to march rapidly to the Delaware River. At the same time, men from Essex, Middlesex, Hunterdon and Somerset were called up as refugees

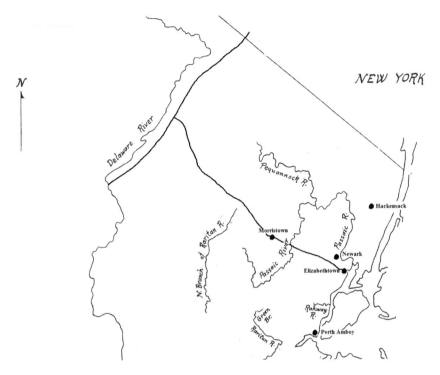

A map of the Military Road constructed during the French and Indian War. *Author's collection.*

flooded in from Pennsylvania from the region around Easton, which had been devastated by the French. New Jersey soon moved to begin the construction of defensive works to secure the colony's exposed borders. The Military Road was constructed under the supervision of Jonathan Hampton of Elizabethtown. Stretching from that city to Sussex County, it was designed to rapidly bring supplies to the region in case of attack. At the same time, portions of the Old Mine Road were built up from Belvidere to Port Jervis, New York. Blockhouses were eventually constructed every eight miles, creating a defensive perimeter around Sussex County and northwestern New Jersey. In addition, a frontier guard was raised to help man the fortifications, with advertisements appearing in many local papers.

> *This is to give notice to all able-bodied freemen, not inhabitants of the county of Sussex, who are willing to enter into the service of the province of New Jersey, in defending the frontier parts of said*

province, that on their application to me the subscriber, at Fort John's or elsewhere in the county of Sussex, they shall immediately be enlisted, and be upon the province pay, at TWO SHILLINGS, Proclamation money, per day.[39]

The troops that had been raised under Schuyler departed for Albany to take part in a planned campaign against Fort Niagara. The Jersey Blues joined with troops from New York and New England and proceeded slowly up the Mohawk River. Governor William Shirley, the commander of the expedition, quickly began to experience difficulties in maintaining his army as it moved through the wilderness of New York. By mid-September, the campaign was called off, and the New Jersey soldiers were used to garrison Fort Oswego. They remained there until December, when they returned home to man the border fortresses that had recently been constructed.

The situation along the Delaware had changed drastically since the departure of troops for the northern theater. When hostilities had erupted, the various native tribes across the Delaware River had borne no hostility to the colony of New Jersey, instead focusing on Pennsylvania and its inhabitants. But now that various militia units had crossed the river to aid the inhabitants of Northampton County, their colony, too, had become a target. A letter from December 1755 exposes the situation in Sussex County: "The country all above this town, for fifty miles is mostly evacuated and ruined, excepting only the neighbourhood of the Depuys five families, which stand their ground...The Enemy made but few prisoners, murdering almost all that fell into their hands."[40] Though the governor and assembly had battled throughout the winter over funding the militia bill, tales such as these sparked bipartisan support for the construction of additional blockhouses along the Sussex County border. The legislation passed by the assembly noted:

Several murders, cruelties and devastations have been lately committed upon His Majesty's subjects in the neighbouring Province of Pennsylvania...in the upper parts of the said Province joining upon the River Delaware and bordering upon this Province of New Jersey, where the said Savages are now daily murdering the inhabitants and burning and destroying all before them, and this even within view of the inhabitants settled along the River Delaware in the County of Sussex, who are quitting their habitations in the utmost confusion.

The act led to the formation of a guard in March 1756 consisting of 250 men whose duty it was to patrol the region and stave off Indian incursions.

The beginning of the offensive season in 1756 again saw the dispatch of the Jersey Blues to Albany due to continued Indian threats and depredations. The force was to be split, with half again being stationed at Fort Oswego under Schuyler and the other half advancing to Schenectady under the command of John Parker. The units sent to Oswego were garrisoned in nearby Fort George, a small, unfinished wooden construction that lacked loopholes, firing platforms and even cannon. In fact, the men recorded that the only way to fire from the fort was to open its front gate.[41] Various diseases brought about by the dung, trash and corpses of the fort reduced the effectiveness of the force from New Jersey as well as the various other English and colonial units.

Over the course of four days, from August 10 to August 14, the French under de Montcalm bombarded the defensives of Oswego. A series of mistakes by the English combined with the gruesome death of Colonel Mercer to compel the surrender of the colonial units. Schuyler and his men were captured and transported to Montreal. Though fifty-seven of the Jersey Blues would be released from Quebec in October, the majority would be held until the following year.

The largest threat to the colony, however, remained natives from across the Delaware, as peace had been established with the various New Jersey tribes at Crosswicks in January 1756. In May, natives raided into Sussex County, assaulting homes at Paulins Kill. Thomas Hunt and his slave were taken captive, while the entire Swartwout family was butchered and scalped. Sixty families quickly fled the region, escaping to Amwell to avoid further attacks. On June 2, for the first and only time in the state's history, New Jersey issued a declaration of war. The Lenni Lenape were declared to be "enemies, rebels, and traitors to his most sacred majesty." A reward of 150 Spanish dollars was offered for any male Indian over the age of fifteen taken alive, $130 for any killed, $150 for rescuing a colonist and $130 for killing a male or female under the age of fifteen. In June, a group of 104 militiamen set out from Paulins Kill, raiding toward the Great Swamp and burning four Indian towns.

The year 1757 saw New Jersey raising more troops and increasing its war debt to over £58,000. In June of that year, additional soldiers were sent to upstate New York to reinforce Fort William Henry. These men would take part in a British probe north of the fort aimed at reconnoitering the French position. Colonel John Parker and his 350 men sailed about twenty miles north of Fort William Henry to land at Sabbath Day Point on the western side of Lake George. On July 21, the French under de Corbiere intercepted three of Parker's boats, which had been sent ahead as scouts. After questioning the men, the French prepared an ambush for the remaining provincial forces. When Parker and his main force neared land, they were instantly attacked by a flotilla of Indians who closed in from the lake. Bullets from the woods along the shore only further spread terror through the ranks of the English as over 100 of the Jersey Blues were killed or drowned while attempting to escape the ambush. Those who made it to shore were then set upon by the waiting French and Indians. Though Parker managed to lead a handful of men to safety, around 160 were led captive back to Fort Carillon, where one unlucky member of the Jersey militia was even boiled and eaten. As recorded by an aide-de-camp to Montcalm, "They put in the pot and ate three prisoners, and perhaps others were so treated. All have become slaves unless they are ransomed. A horrible spectacle to European eyes."[42] The remains of the men from the Garden State were still visible a year later to the men of General Abercromby's army while en route to Fort Carillon.

The French followed up their victory in August with Montcalm's seizure of Fort William Henry. Over 2,300 English and colonial soldiers were taken prisoner, and in the famous massacre that followed, over 100 were butchered by the Algonquin allies of the French. Colonel Parker and the survivors of Sabbath Day Point were captured and held as prisoners by the French for a year and a half. One unlucky member of the Jersey Blues, Sergeant William McCracken, would not return home until August 1763, having been held in a series of French prisons and then pressed into service on a British warship upon his initial release. The release of Peter Schuyler from his own imprisonment after the fall of Oswego was celebrated in Newark with bonfires, cannonades, fireworks and drinking. Famed early American poet Annis Boudinot Stockton published a poem in the *New York Mercury* on January 9, 1758, to mark the occasion:

> *DEAR to each Muse, and to thy Country dear,*
> *Welcome once more to breathe thy native Air;*
> *Not half so cheering is the solar Ray,*

To the harsh Rigour of a Winter's Day;
Not half so grateful fanning Breezes rise,
When the hot Dog Star burns the Summer Skies;
CAESARAE's Shore with Acclamation rings,
And, Welcome SCHUYLER, every shepherd sings.
See for thy Brows, the Laurel is prepar'd,
And justly deem'd, a PATRIOT thy Reward;
Ev'n future Ages shall enroll thy Name,
In sacred Annals of immortal Fame.

Further alarms of Indian attacks along the frontier led the assembly to vote funding for fifty additional soldiers on October 22, 1757. Yet by June of the following year, over forty additional residents of the colony had been massacred by Native Americans. In one such attack, a local man named William Ward was struck down while hunting only a half mile from a manned fort. On May 17, four members of the Cole family along with three Germans were massacred by a group of natives. Soldiers from Fort Normanock set out to rescue Cole's wife and son, ambushing the Indians responsible.

In response, the assembly on August 12, 1758, authorized the raising of an additional 150 men as well as fifty dogs to help track and attack the Indians. A series of nine forts and four ranging posts were eventually constructed from Warren County to Port Jervis. Among these were Fort Reading in Belvidere, Fort Ellison in Knowlton and New Fort by Columbia, all of which were along the Delaware River. The line of fortifications then continued along the Old Mine Road winding into Sussex County. The first of these was Van Campen's house, a prominent structure in the region, followed by Fort Walpack, Adam Dingman's Fort, Van Campen's Inn, Carmer's Fort at the juncture of Old Mine and Walpack Roads, Fort Nominack at Sandyston, Fort Shipeconk or Brinks and Cole's Fort in Port Jervis. The vast majority of these consisted of simple blockhouses surrounded by wooden palisades, the ruins of many of which are still partially visible in the region. Fort John's, built near Van Campen's Inn, served as the headquarters for New Jersey troops in the area.

It was during this war along its northwestern frontier that the province of New Jersey handed out its only ever medals for bravery. Sergeant John van Tile and a young boy named Titfort each received a silver medal the size of a dollar engraved with a prostrate Indian. The assembly

A picture of the Van Campen house, which served as a fort along the Delaware River. *Library of Congress.*

encouraged both men to wear their awards at all public ceremonies so as to "kindle a Martial Fire in the Breast of the Spectators, so truly essential in this Time of general War."[43]

In October 1758, the colony of New Jersey officially made peace with the surrounding Native American tribes. At a conference held in Easton, Pennsylvania, representatives of the major Indian nations, the English Crown and the colonies of Pennsylvania and New Jersey met and agreed to a peace deal. The natives pledged to no longer attack the English in exchange for hunting grounds in the Ohio region. At the same time, the Lenape surrendered all claims to lands in New Jersey in exchange for 1,000 Spanish dollars. Shortly after, Edgepelick (later renamed Brotherton) was established in Burlington County as perhaps the first Indian reservation in America.

That same year, the colony of New Jersey organized another expedition toward the New York frontier. Permanent barracks were constructed in Perth Amboy, New Brunswick, Elizabeth, Trenton and Burlington to end the practice of the British quartering in colonial homes. Once completed, the barracks in Trenton was the largest building in the city and would remain a center of military life for a century. In addition, following an appearance by the Earl of Loudon, the British commander-in-chief for North America, the assembly issued a call for one thousand additional men. An additional £50,000 was also approved in March 1758 due to Prime Minister Pitt's assurances that the money would be refunded once the war was won. The province would provide the raised soldiers with a coat, breeches, a checkered shirt, two pairs of shoes, two pairs of stockings, a hat, a blanket, a canteen, a hatchet, a bounty of £12, pay of £1.13.6 per month and a dollar to "drink to his majesty's health." The *New York Mercury* could rightfully say that the Jersey Blues were "the likeliest well set men for the purpose as have perhaps been turned out on any campaign."[44] Meanwhile, Governor Francis Bernard could rightly gloat that "these men are sent into the field in a different manner from those of most other provinces: they are completely clothed in a handsome uniform and furnished with all necessaries, and they are mustered to a man in both which articles several of the other provinces are greatly deficient."[45]

In May, this well-dressed regiment of Jersey Blues set out for Albany under Colonel John Johnson. From there, they would join other colonial troops and British regulars for an assault on Fort Ticonderoga. Yet for all of its pomp and promise, the offensive was a resounding failure. General Abercrombie's direct assault on the fort was driven off by stiff French resistance. The New Jersey soldiers were thrown into combat at the last moment, and though they did not suffer heavy casualties, their concerted efforts did not breach the French defenses. The troops soon dispersed and returned home with little to show from the campaign season.

Over the next few years, the colony would repeat the process of recruiting men and sending them to the New York frontier. Bounties were offered, additional recruiting stations and barracks were opened and, once again, Peter Schuyler was placed in command of New Jersey forces. The British began to rely more and more on colonial forces as garrison units, allowing them to employ regular troops elsewhere. In 1760 alone, units from New Jersey were stationed at Fort Oswego and employed a band of rangers in the area. While the year before, a party of 16 Jersey Blues was ambushed by 240 French allied Indians near Lake George. The natives "killed and scalped six, wounded two, took four prisoners, and only four of the whole party escaped. They shewed [*sic*] themselves plainly to the whole Army after they got the scalps, gave a hollow, and then made off to their Battoes, which were not more than two miles from the Head of the Lake. A large party was

The Old Barracks of Trenton, erected during the French and Indian Wars and used by New Jersey troops for over two hundred years. *New Jersey Historical Society.*

ordered out after them, but in vain. They butchered our people in a most shocking manner, by cutting pieces of flesh out of their necks, thighs and legs."[46]

In 1762, troops from the province again took part in another British assault on the sugar islands of the Caribbean. In June of that year, George Keppel, the third Earl of Albemarle, landed thousands of British soldiers outside Havana, Cuba. Yellow fever decimated the ranks of the English as their siege lines slowly strangled the city. By July, half the army was incapacitated. The end of the month saw colonial reinforcements arrive from Connecticut, New York, Rhode Island and New Jersey in an attempt to help secure the port and island. On August 13, after two months of fighting, the city of Havana finally fell to the British. In the end, over twice as many men would die from disease than from combat. The Jersey Blues had taken part in another successful foreign adventure for the British Crown. Yet in the end, the island was quickly returned to Spanish control, with perhaps the only tangible result for New Jersey besides casualties being a four-pounder bronze Spanish cannon now housed at the Old Barracks in Trenton.

Though the ending of the French and Indian Wars secured control of the majority of North America for the British, it little benefited the people of New Jersey. An estimated three thousand men, perhaps one-quarter of the non-Quaker adult male population of the state, served in the conflict, yet only debt and factionalism emerged as the biggest spoils of war for the colony.[47] A century of warfare had brought out the best and worst in the colony and paved the way for its eventual independence.

NEW JERSEY LINE WAR

France and Spain weren't the only enemies faced by New Jersey during the colonial era. A sixty-year conflict highlighted by arguments, kidnappings and gun battles raged between the provinces of New Jersey and New York over their respective boundaries. The separation of New Jersey from New York in 1665 had deprived the latter of very productive farmland and mines. However, the lack of an understood boundary between the two colonies would lead to repeated land sales, double taxation and odious militia requirements.

By the turn of the eighteenth century, disputes over properties along the border turned violent. Farmers raided one another's lands, burned crops, stoned houses, stole possessions and assaulted one another. Two of the more colorful families involved were the Swartwouts of New York and the Westfalls of New Jersey. War officially erupted between the two in 1718 when, on a moonlight night, Johannes Westfall and his men attempted to attack the cornfields of Jacobus Swartwout. Informed of the raid, Swartwout and his men were already present, and a drunken brawl soon ensued. The two patriarchs even took part in a bizarre pumpkin-throwing duel, after which both sides quickly retreated.

Events took a more serious turn in 1738 when one violent raid by the Westfalls resulted in the death of Major Philip Swartwout's wife. She perished a few days after the attack, having already been in ill health at the time. While the major was away at a town meeting that fall, the Westfalls again assaulted and seized his house. Swartwout later organized a successful counterattack and drove the New Jersey men back over the border, delivering "three or four hearty kicks upon the ringleader's rear as a parting admonition when he stepped from the door."[48] Two further invasions by forces from New Jersey failed, leading to the death of a horse but no other casualties.

As the war intensified, the authorities of both states slowly became involved, issuing warrants and arresting various residents. After arresting a New York resident, New Jersey justice of the peace Solomon Davis was himself arrested on a warrant issued by Orange County. Davis was finally released after paying a £40 fine. Another justice of the peace, Abraham Vanaken, was soon arrested as well, while another constable had his horse shot out from under him by a group of New Yorkers before being dragged off to a prison.

In August 1754, a band of Westfalls assaulted Samuel Finch, an Orange County constable, in his shop in Minisink. After Finch refused to go with them, the men dragged him through the swamp, seriously injuring him. Only the arrival of another New York justice allowed for the rescue of the injured man. In retaliation, New Jersey Quaker John Herring was beaten by an Orange County justice named Tom Dekay and his sons.

The next year, a party of Westfalls again assaulted the property of Major Philip Swartwout. Petrus Smoke, the sheriff of Sussex County, along with eleven other men evicted Swartwout, seized his goods and forced him to become a lessee on his own property. The family lived in a small kitchen for the next four years until 1759, when the sheriff of Orange County was sent by the president of the King's Council to return the land to Swartwout. Yet he was again arrested two years later and brought to a Sussex County jail, only to be released upon payment of a £1,600 bail bond. One of the last recorded attacks occurred in 1765 when a party of men from Sussex County attempted to kidnap Swartwout and others from the Old Dutch Church in Port Jervis during services. Since it was a Sunday, both sides agreed to forgo guns and resorted to fisticuffs.

By 1769, King George III had dispatched commissioners to settle the dispute. After much research and surveying, the border was finalized between the two provinces in 1772, with New Jersey losing some 210,000 acres. Westfall lands in particular were split, with a substantial amount being assigned to Orange County.

CHAPTER 3

CROSSROADS OF THE REVOLUTION: NEW JERSEY AND THE FIGHT FOR INDEPENDENCE

Due to its geographic location, straddling the Northern and Southern Colonies, occupying the transportation network that connected New York City and the Revolutionary capital at Philadelphia and hugging the trade routes along the coast, New Jersey was destined to become the pivot point around which campaigns of the Revolution revolved. Beyond the traditionally studied campaigns of 1776 and 1777 within the Garden State, the province played a vital role in supplying the rebel army as well as harassing the British at sea. Many ordinary residents of the region gave everything for a chance at liberty, complementing the heroic actions of their brothers, fathers and sons in the state's militia. The state would see both the high and low points of the conflict, and it would experience almost constant fighting between 1776 and the end of the war, longer than almost any other region.

ROAD TO WAR

The road to the Revolution for New Jersey began well before most other colonies. Anger over the rising number of debtors in the colony, as well as battles over landownership that had been raging for the last century, created a tension in the province toward London rivaled only by that in Massachusetts. The previous chapter has already detailed the various land riots that took place across the region beginning in the 1740s and the periodic rebellions against various royal governors from the early days of the colony. The increased pain felt by the growing debtor class within New Jersey resulted in the rise of the Liberty Boys movement by the 1760s, a local version of the Sons of Liberty. Barn burnings by the group, as well as other forms of civil and uncivil disobedience, became rampant by 1770.

Chapters of the group had formed a few years before in response to the Stamp Act crisis then sweeping the colonies. While proclaiming loyalty to King George III, members set about employing sabotage and economic boycotts to protest the new taxes, committing "our lives and fortunes in the defense of our liberties and privileges."[49] Though General Gage offered the governor of New Jersey one hundred soldiers to enforce the law and suppress the Liberty Boys, William Franklin decided against the move that would have undoubtedly led to an escalation of violence, much as it did in Massachusetts. The repeal of the hated tax only a short time later led to an explosion of celebration throughout the colonies. The *New York Mercury* reported that in Sussex County alone, one thousand Liberty Boys gathered at the courthouse to celebrate the tax's demise.

Subsequent taxes by the British led to further riots and protests in the colonies. The infamous tea tax granted by Parliament to bolster the British East India Company led to some of the most famous incidents of resistance in New Jersey and elsewhere. In January 1774, only a few weeks after the more well-known Boston Tea Party, students at Princeton performed their own nocturnal raid. According to one student at the time, the young men "gathered all the steward's winter store of tea and having made a fire on the campus we there burned near a dozen pound, tolled the bell, and made many spirited resolves."[50] The governor of Massachusetts, Thomas Hutchinson, was then burned in effigy with a tea canister around his neck outside Nassau Hall. Groups of students dressed all in white ranged the town, seizing and burning quantities of tea held by private citizens. But this wasn't the only incident of resistance on the campus. Four years earlier, students had publicly burned a letter in the college yard from a group of New York merchants requesting that Philadelphia abandon its adherence to the non-importation movement then popular in the colonies. A young James Madison, after witnessing the event, wrote to his father that "Their Letter to the Merchants in Philadelphia...was latley burnt by the Students of this place in the college Yard, all of them appearing in their black Gowns and the bell Tolling."[51]

Nearly a year after the Princeton Tea Party, a larger one took place farther south at Greenwich. A few months before, during the summer of 1774, the ship *Greyhound* had unsuccessfully tried to unload its cargo of tea in Philadelphia. Unable to do so, the captain of the small ship sailed up Cohansey Creek and removed his merchandise to the house of Daniel Bowen, a Loyalist in Greenwich, where it remained for almost five months. On the night of December 22, a group of forty men dressed as Indians burst into Bowen's home, removed the tea and burned it in a nearby field. Though a countywide committee meeting the next day condemned the action, many participants of the raid were on the committee itself, and no subsequent legal action was taken. The Greenwich Tea Burning remains as one of the four most well-known tea parties to take place in the colonies and included such future Patriots and leaders as Silas Newcomb (a general in the New Jersey militia) and Richard Howell (future governor of the state).

THE WAR AT SEA

One of the state's most memorable and earliest contributions to the fight for independence was in the realm of privateering. Since the first wars for North America fought between the British and French, the coast of New Jersey had been a hotbed for the raiding of merchantmen. Thus, the early occurrences of privateering that filled the waters off the Jersey shore during the war should come as no surprise.

In January 1775, three months before the opening of hostilities at Lexington and Concord, a British army supply ship was taken off Sandy Hook, with its cargo sold publicly in Elizabethtown. Once fighting did erupt in Massachusetts, naval warfare along the Jersey coastline became endemic. Only weeks after the firing of the shot heard 'round the world, a British warship even attempted to raid Greenwich for cattle.

Various English warships and merchantmen beached while attempting to sail the unfamiliar coastline during the conflict. Militiamen from the coastal counties were usually quick to respond to such occurrences. As early as October 15, 1775, the English transport *Rebecca & Francis* ran aground at Brigantine Beach. Men of the Egg Harbor Guard, part of the Gloucester County militia, under Colonel Richard Somers, captured the crew and proceeded to reduce the ship to ashes. Perhaps most notable was the floundering of the *Love and Unity*, which grounded in August 1778 near Toms River. Over eighty hogsheads of loaf sugar, thousands of bottles of porter and beer and other supplies were recovered from the hold. The ship was eventually repaired, refloated and renamed by its new owners as the *Washington*.

Egg Harbor in particular became a nest of privateering action during the war. Ships like the *Congress* and the *Chance* prowled the waterways of the Jersey shore from that port, capturing numerous warships and merchantmen. Off the coast of New Jersey alone, over one hundred engagements are recorded as having taken place between privateers and English ships from 1778 to 1783.[52]

The names of many notable privateers exist within New Jersey history and folklore. Micajah Smith and David Stevens, captains of the *Sly* and *Chance*, respectively, achieved fame with their capture of the English ship *Venus* in August 1778. Considered to be one of the most valuable prizes taken in the war, the ship brought in £17,609 at auction, with its cable and anchor alone fetching £1,500. The privateers not only sought merchantmen and treasure but also engaged warships and sought to disrupt military operations. In this vein, in September 1779, Yelverton Taylor of the *Mars* captured the British ship *Triton*, which was carrying a company of Hessians to reinforce Clinton in New York. Yet not all the encounters between the privateers and the English ended in death or capture. A legendary encounter occurred in the case of Edward Giles of the *Shark*, who, after being captured by the British, got his captors drunk and managed to retake his vessel from them in their inebriated state.

A large privateering base was eventually constructed by Colonel John Cox of Batsto Village at Chestnut Neck near Port Republic. After the fall of New York and Philadelphia, the port became the nexus of a supply route bringing much-needed food, clothing and ammunition to the Continentals camped at Valley Forge. Its importance did not escape the notice of the British, and in late September 1778, Sir Henry Clinton dispatched a fleet of nine ships and transports under Captain Henry Collins, along with 300 British regulars and 100 New Jersey Loyalists under Captain Patrick Ferguson, to destroy the port and clear the region of privateers. Clearly understanding the importance of the base, Washington dispatched Casmir Pulaski with 333 men to reinforce the privateers and militiamen. Foul weather and the local sandbar conspired to delay the British attack for days. Yet the 200 Patriots present at Chestnut Neck quickly withdrew from the breastworks after the initial English landing, knowing the futility of their position. Collins recovered ten vessels, including the *Venus*, burning them and the storehouses before withdrawing to the mouth of the Bass River, where the saltworks, mills and home of Eli Mathias were likewise razed to the ground. Luckily, in the end, the warning provided by Governor Livingston and others allowed the privateers to save themselves, their goods and most of their vessels. The operation produced little lasting benefit for the British as the New Jersey privateers were soon back at sea harassing the shipping lanes around New York City.

Count Pulaski did eventually arrive on October 8, at which point he marched to Tuckerton, where his men and those of Collins observed one another for almost a week. On the fifteenth, in a surprise night raid, Captain Ferguson led English soldiers and New Jersey Loyalists in an attack on a fifty-man Patriot outpost. The majority were massacred in their sleep after Ferguson allegedly gave the order for no quarter to be given. The Massacre of Little Egg Harbor did much to further stiffen attitudes between Patriots and Loyalists within the state. One of the legends of the origin of the Jersey Devil revolves around a Leeds Point girl who had a child with a British soldier after the Battle of Chestnut Neck. Cursed for breeding with an Englishman, her child was born an abomination.[53]

It was only a matter of time before large-scale naval engagements also took place in the waters off New Jersey. Over the course of a year and a half, the USS *Lexington* in particular engaged British warships, privateers and merchantmen off the shores of New Jersey and Delaware. Perhaps its most notable engagement occurred on June 29, 1776, off the coast of Cape May. What became known as the Battle of Turtle Gut Inlet started with the flight of the brig *Nancy*, which was carrying gunpowder and supplies from the Caribbean to the rebelling colonies. Pursued by six British ships, the *Nancy* grounded itself in Cape May under the cover of heavy fog. Captain John Barry, the father of the American navy, brought the *Lexington, Wasp* and *Reprisal* to the scene to aid the stricken ship. Throughout the night, men from all four craft unloaded over 260 barrels of desperately needed gunpowder from the *Nancy*, all while under bombardment from the British. As the enemy finally boarded the craft late in the morning, the booby-trapped ship exploded, blowing the

English "forty or fifty feet into the air."[54] The successful unloading of the vast majority of supplies was considered a victory by the Americans, yet it did not come without loss. Lieutenant Richard Wickes, brother of the captain of the *Reprisal*, was killed during the battle, representing the first casualty on New Jersey soil during the war.

Sandy Hook represented a natural target for both sides during the course of the war. Controlling access to Lower New York Bay, it saw numerous naval battles between the British and Americans. These attacks began as early as 1775, when the HMS *Viper* captured at least two ships in the area, and stretched until December 1782, when the American ship *Greyhound* captured the British ships *Diamond* and *Dolphin*.

A more important aspect of the spit of land for the two sides, though, was the Sandy Hook Lighthouse. Built in 1764 following the raising of concerns by a group of New York merchants, the structure remains the oldest standing lighthouse in the nation. Acknowledged early on in the war as vital to the effective control of the region, it became a target for both sides. Congress ordered Major William Malcolm in March 1776 to "take the glass out of the lantern…use your best discretion to render the lighthouse entirely useless." Loyalist governor of New York William Tryon likewise ordered the pilothouse on Sandy Hook to be burned in April. With the onset of Howe's invasion of New York City, the peninsula and its lighthouse became a valuable target for the British. By June 1776, only three months after Malcolm's dismantling of the light, the English had possession of the structure and had returned it to working order. Lieutenant Colonel William Tupper, who had previously sabotaged Boston Light to hinder English operations in that area, was dispatched by Washington to destroy the Sandy Hook Lighthouse. Unfortunately, the solid construction of the building foiled his efforts, as his cannonballs were unable to penetrate the edifice. Over the next year, three different rebel attempts were made by upward of three hundred men to assault the building, but each ended in failure. As the war progressed, the area was used as a refugee camp for Tories and escaped slaves, many of whom began raiding into New Jersey in coordination with British efforts, most notably against Shrewsbury in March 1780. In that same year, Captain Michael Rudolph, who had been brevetted for his heroism at Paulus Hook in 1779, raided the camp, capturing seven men and, more importantly, netting 45,000 counterfeit Continental dollars.

Rudolph's operation was part of Washington's larger campaign of countering British efforts to destroy the American economy via counterfeiting of the new nation's currency. American raids would continue against the area almost up to the end of the war.

THE FALL OF NEW JERSEY

Though major fighting would not reach the territory of New Jersey until 1776, the province was already preparing for conflict years prior. In 1774, students at Princeton were already forming military companies to train for commissions in the expected war. In the spring of 1775, three battalions of soldiers were helping General Philip Schuyler guard Lake Champlain. By the fall, the new provisional congress had raised the First and Second New Jersey Regiments under William Alexander, better known as Lord Stirling, and William Maxwell, respectively. Many of these soldiers were soon called on to help disarm Tories on Long Island, as General Washington feared their presence so near to his forces. Colonel Nathan Heard's success in this operation led to a local tune among Tories:

> *Colonel Heard has come to town,*
> *In all his pride and glory.*
> *And when he dies he'll go to hell,*
> *For robbing of the Tory.*

War finally came to New Jersey in 1776 with the opening of General Howe's New York Campaign. Two additional regiments were raised in the colony—the Third and Fourth—and on March 26, the Committee on Public Safety dispatched two thousand soldiers to New York City under Generals Dickinson and Livingston. Unfortunately, due to a lack of supplies, the battalions were ordered to "impress arms" if necessary in order to prepare themselves for battle.[55] In addition, batteries were established at various points in New Jersey ringing New York City, including at Perth Amboy and at Paulus Hook, while Fort Constitution (later renamed Fort Lee) was constructed overlooking Burdett's Landing on the Hudson River. Washington positioned his troops at strategic locations around New York Bay, including a Flying Camp at Perth Amboy under General Hugh Mercer that consisted of ten thousand men from the Middle Colonies.

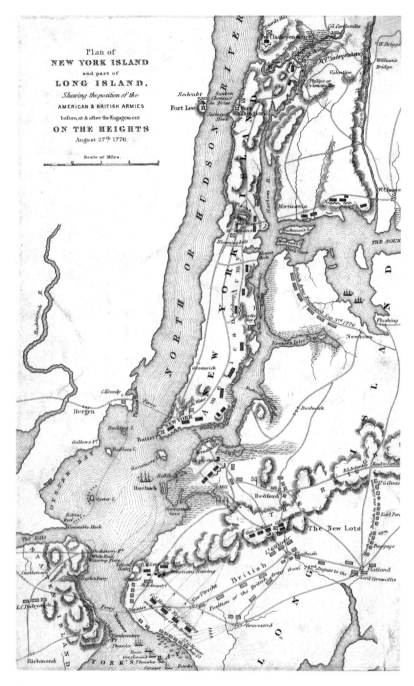

The positions of American and English forces on the eve of the Battle of Brooklyn. *Library of Congress.*

Though Howe arrived in New York Bay in July 1776, he delayed his assault on the city until the arrival of Clinton and Cornwallis with an additional ten thousand men in August. In the meantime, various bombardments and raids characterized the first month of the Battle of New York. British cannons on Staten Island and American pieces in Perth Amboy periodically exchanged fire. Damaged headstones still remain in the graveyard of St. Peter's Church in Perth Amboy, where a rebel cannon was located, as a testament to the skirmish. Later that same month, the British warships HMS *Phoenix* and HMS *Rose* likewise took part in an artillery duel with New Jersey batteries at Paulus Hook. As Howe's planned assault on New York City grew closer, probing raids were launched by both sides. On July 10, a British attempt to land at Elizabethtown was driven off by local militia, while eight days later, a similar assault by Mercer from Perth Amboy against Staten Island was prevented by poor weather.

The Battle of Long Island proved to be a rout for the Continental army. Yet the leadership of various officers and the bravery of the men in the field allowed for Washington to safely extricate his army, even though he lost the island. In particular, New Jersey's Lord Stirling's dogged defense of the Gowanis Road secured the right flank of the American force, and though it led to his capture by the British, he helped garner for his Maryland troopers and their province the nickname of the Old Line State. Likewise. Colonel Heard's New Jersey brigade suffered heavily defending the area of Flatbush Road. One of his colonels, Philip Johnston, was even killed helping to hold back the British advance.

As Washington slowly withdrew through Manhattan, the British began to periodically bombard the entrenched artillery batteries at Paulus Hook. Though an English assault on the rebel positions was driven off on September 21, a second attack two days later succeeded. The British had secured for themselves their first piece of New Jersey, a colony in which they would retain a foothold until the end of the war. While the English were advancing upward from Manhattan and slowly securing Bergen County, the Flying Camp under Mercer at Perth Amboy remained relatively inactive. Raids by Matthias Williamson and Hugh Mercer in mid-October against Staten Island netted a few prisoners, yet the boredom that raged in the camp led to increased desertions as the fall wore on.

As Washington's retreat took him over the Hudson River and into New Jersey, it was only a matter of time before the English army followed him. The general watched on November 16 from Fort Lee as Fort Washington across the Hudson surrendered to Von Knyphausen. It was now simply a matter of time before Howe sent his army over the Hudson to pursue the Americans across New Jersey, advancing ever closer toward the new capital at Philadelphia. As Tory raiding parties roamed the various towns and villages of Bergen County, Cornwallis was readying 2,500 men to cross the river and assault Fort Lee. This invasion force aimed at not only seizing Fort Lee but also surrounding and finishing off Washington's army, thus removing the only substantial force between Howe and Philadelphia.

Two small incidents conspired to save both Washington's defeated army and perhaps the fate of the Revolution as well. While a Bergen County Tory named John Aldington was directing Cornwallis and his twelve regiments up the cliffs of the Palisades, an unnamed horseman known to history only as the Closter Horseman was galloping south toward Fort Lee to warn the militia and General Nathanael Greene of the approaching army. Despite the general's posting of lookouts throughout the area, he apparently had been unaware of the landing.[56] Washington ordered the rebel army to withdraw, and General Greene with around one thousand men and famed Patriot Thomas Paine in tow marched out of the fort and toward Hackensack. Paine recorded, "Our situation there was exceedingly cramped…our force was inconsiderable…we had no army at hand to have relieved the garrison, had we shut ourselves up and stood on our defence [*sic*]. Our ammunition, light artillery, and the best part of our stores, had been removed."[57] At the same time, the British failed to secure the New Bridge over the Hackensack River, allowing for an orderly withdrawal by the Americans. Thanks to these mistakes by the British and strokes of good fortune for the rebels, the only sizeable Continental force between New York City and Philadelphia was saved. Paine himself wrote, "Howe, in my little opinion, committed a great error in generalship in not throwing a body of forces off from Staten Island through Amboy, by which means he might have seized all our stores at Brunswick, and intercepted our march into Pennsylvania."[58]

Washington and Greene combined forces at Hackensack and proceeded on their slow, orderly withdrawal through New Jersey. On November 21, the Patriots destroyed the bridge over the Acquackanonk River to slow down their British pursuers. Washington had hoped to confront the English next at Newark, but his numerical inferiority prevented this. Residents of the city panicked as the enemy approached, hiding their goods and fleeing from their homes. The American retreat was heavily hampered by the ending of many of the militia's terms of service. By the time Washington reached New Brunswick, the Flying Camp had largely dispersed and most of his Maryland and New Jersey regiments disbanded. The bridge over the Raritan was only partially destroyed, and an artillery duel across the river soon commenced. Only Howe's ordering of Cornwallis to await his arrival saved the American force from again being cornered. The retreat continued, and by December 8, the last of Washington's troops crossed the Delaware into Pennsylvania. Hessians occupied Trenton, while Cornwallis initially withdrew to Pennington.

Civilians in the state also suffered during the British advance. Refugees began fleeing from towns, while others prepared for the horrors of occupation. The state government, having only just recently elected a governor, disbanded and fled. Speaker John Hart returned home to Hopewell to find his house ransacked, his wife dead and his children scattered. Richard Stockton, one of the signers of the Declaration, was captured by Loyalists and turned over to the British. Held for weeks, Stockton was harshly treated in confinement and spent years recovering his health. To avoid similar ravages during the occupation of Princeton, President John Witherspoon, himself a signer, ordered the evacuation of the College of New Jersey.

Pardons were offered to any New Jersey residents who took an oath of allegiance to the king within sixty days, with around 2,700 doing so, according to reports from General Howe. This is confirmed in a letter from Matthias Williamson to Washington, which reads, "I am sorry to say that altho [*sic*] there was great necessity for them to exert themselves at this important Crisis, very few of the Counties of Essex or Bergen join'd my Command. At this Time, I have no Influence in either of those Counties, but have it from good Intelligence that many who bore the Character of warm Whigs have been foremost in seeking protection from Genl Howe and forsaking the American Cause."[59]

Yet far from attempting to win over the hearts and minds of the people, the British and Hessians proceeded to ravage the state. Robbery, rape and murder became rampant against both Patriots and those who sought pardons. Elizabethtown soon became a tremendous depot for the ill-gotten gains of the English. Princeton, as a center of rebel activity and the location of a major British camp, became a particularly hard-hit town. The homes of various leaders of the state were plundered or burned, while Nassau Hall at Princeton was ransacked. The college contained what was considered at the time to be the most advanced planetarium in North America or Europe. The damage to the equipment was extensive and was not fully repaired until years after the Revolution.[60] Once the English were firmly in control of the province, Tories likewise emerged and began to target and pillage their Patriot neighbors.

LOYALISTS AND TORIES

The War for Independence was sometimes less of a revolution than it was a civil war. As in many of the other colonies, the population of New Jersey was split between loyalty to the Crown and desire for independence. Tories were most active in the northeastern areas of the state, especially among the Dutch families of Bergen and the Germans of Hunterdon. With the impending arrival of Howe in New York, various Tory groups began assaulting their Patriot neighbors and raiding various parts of the state. On June 24, 1776, a group of Loyalists in Hunterdon County under John Vought launched a raid against Jones Tavern in Sidney (modern-day Clinton). Armed with clubs, the Tories raided the militia recruiting station and sought to intimidate the local militia officer, Captain Thomas Jones. Angered by the assault, a group of militiamen under Colonel Frederick Frelinghuysen were dispatched by the Provincial Congress a few weeks later to arrest Vought. After being fined, John and his father, Stoffel, were released, only to become more devoted Loyalists.

The Voughts were not alone in their opposition to independence, and the arrival of General Howe off the coast of New Jersey proved to be a call to arms for Tories throughout the state. Uprisings in Hunterdon County necessitated the calling out of the state militia, while Loyalists in Shrewsbury refused to comply with the orders of the Provincial Congress. By July, Monmouth was said to be teeming with pro-British activity, including the notorious Pine Robbers of the coast. Citizens of the state, eager to show their support for the Crown, flocked to the English banner on Staten Island. Two notable Tories, Elisha Lawrence and John Morris, even rowed out to Howe's fleet in a small rowboat, promising to raise loyal regiments.

Once Howe was firmly in control of New York City, he authorized Cortlandt Skinner, the former Speaker of the House and attorney general of New Jersey, to raise a series of regiments within the state. These six battalions, known as Skinner's Greens due to the color of their uniforms, were raised mostly from Sussex, Bergen, Essex, Hunterdon and Monmouth. Though not thought of highly by the British regulars, they performed garrison duties and provided valuable knowledge of the land and its citizens. By 1778, former New Jersey governor William Franklin was presiding over the Board of Associated Loyalists in New York City, which helped to recruit and organize the actions of Tories behind the lines in New Jersey.

Many prominent Loyalists existed within the state, and their feats and depredations have become legendary. Prominent among these was Joe Mulliner, the storied Robin Hood of the Pine Barrens. Active around the Mullica River from 1779 onward, Mulliner raided and pillaged the property of prominent Patriots for years. Once, during an attack on the home of the widow Bates, one of his men burned the house to the ground. The gentlemanly Mulliner sent a written apology along with $300 to the old woman, earning him the grudging respect of some of the locals. The outlaw Tory was infamous as well for abducting young ladies from parties, including Honoria Reed, daughter of Charles Reed, the ironmaster of Batsto Village. Ultimately, it was this type of activity that led to his death. In the summer of 1781, Mulliner was captured after crashing a party at Indian Cabin Mill Inn on Nesco Road in Mullica. He was subsequently tried and hanged on Gallows Hill in modern-day Laurel Hill Cemetery. His remains and the location of his grave became something of a tourist attraction for years after his death.

Another famous Loyalist of the region was Titus Cornelius, better known as Colonel Tye. A former slave from Monmouth County, Tye escaped to Virginia after the issuance of the Dunmore Proclamation in 1775. Around 1778, he returned to New Jersey to head the Black Brigade, a small band of fighters who terrorized the region of Monmouth. After participating in the Battle of Monmouth, Tye and his men began to raid the homes of Patriots, assassinating or capturing various leaders in the state. The successes of his actions encouraged more slaves to flee to New York City and offer their services to the English. In response, Governor Livingston ordered a massive manhunt to find Colonel Tye. In 1780, Tye and his men besieged the home of famed New Jersey Patriot Joshua Huddy. After a two-hour firefight, the Loyalists captured Huddy after setting the house ablaze. During the battle, Tye was shot through the wrist, a wound that would eventually lead to either tetanus or gangrene and ultimately his death.

A final famous New Jersey Tory was Captain John Bacon, one of the Robbers of the Pine Barrens. He became known for his particularly bloody attacks against various Patriots and privateers in the state. On December 1, 1780, Bacon and a band of Tories raided Cranberry Inlet, killing Joshua Studson, who had captured the ships *John* and *Catherine* a few months before. Bacon participated in his most infamous assault on October 25, 1782, in what became known as the Long Beach (or Barnegat Light) Massacre. Captain Andrew Steelman and his crew from the *Alligator* had just finished plundering a beached ship and were camping for the night on the beach when Bacon and his band appeared and stabbed to death the captain and twenty-five of his men. It would not be until April 3, 1783, that the Tory was finally tracked down and killed near Tuckerton.

RETAKING NEW JERSEY

The campaign to retake New Jersey began immediately after its fall. As Cornwallis was settling into winter quarters across the state, small-scale guerrilla attacks were already taking place, with General Howe himself even being shot at by some farmers on one occasion. On December 11, 1776, a raid by some New Jersey militiamen netted four hundred cattle and two hundred sheep near Woodbridge, valuable resources for the long winter to come.

At the same time, General William Heath, who had been posted along the Hudson River, was left behind as Washington's retreating army was making its way through the state. To support the withdrawal, his force began to harass various Loyalist units then rising up within New Jersey as well as English regulars. On December 14, Heath surprised a small British unit at Hackensack, taking sixty prisoners, while an ambush at Ringoes on the same day led to the death of a British coronet. Farther south, two hundred of his men performed a raid into Bergen Woods, capturing twenty-three Tories who were forming a Loyalist battalion. By December 16, Heath was pushing through Paramus, attacking English sympathizers as he went.

Washington Crossing the Delaware by Emanuel Leutze. *Metropolitan Museum of Art.*

Despite these attacks, the onset of winter found the British settling into quarters and slowly reducing their footprint in the state. Howe had returned to New York City, while Clinton was dispatched to Newport with six thousand men, and Cornwallis was preparing to sail to England to be with his ailing wife. Hessian units were posted in Trenton and Bordentown, while the British regulars were camped at Princeton and New Brunswick. The German soldiers at Bordentown were under the command of Carl von Donop, an experienced Hessian soldier who had been unable to occupy his preferred site of Burlington due to Commodore Thomas Seymour's constant patrolling of the Delaware River with a Pennsylvania naval squadron. An independent command of Germans under Colonel Johann Rall was billeted in the barracks of Trenton constructed during the French and Indian War.

Washington was in need of a victory to raise the morale of his dispirited troops, to quiet the concerns of Congress and to draw off British strength from attacking other regions. To accomplish this, he began to formulate an attack in late December 1776 aimed at crossing the Delaware River and assaulting the Hessian camp in Trenton.

A few days before General Washington launched his offensive, a separate force of New Jersey and Pennsylvania militia under Samuel Griffin was assaulting Mount Holly. On December 21, Griffin's six hundred men scattered a contingent of the British Forty-second at Petticoat Bridge.

Von Donop responded by pursuing the American force, defeating them at Petticoat Bridge and chasing them through Mount Holly. Though the Battle of Iron Works Hill was a failure for the Americans, it did draw the Hessians farther away from Rall's force at Trenton. Von Donop himself became infatuated with the widow of a local doctor, staying in town until well after the Battle of Trenton. While later stories credit Betsy Ross as being the woman of the story, the importance of the episode lies in the diversion it created, which benefited Washington's famed crossing of the Delaware. As the future president himself opined, "Now is the time to clip their wings while they are so spread."[61]

Soldiers and militiamen continued to depart from Washington's army with alarming speed. By December, following the arrival of reinforcements under Benedict Arnold from Schuyler and Sullivan in New York, the rebels could field six thousand men. Unfortunately, Charles Lee, the leader of the force and one of Washington's chief generals, had been captured by the English on December 12 at Basking Ridge, having taken a leisurely approach to the Patriot camp.

The plan for the battle involved a three-pronged attack on the Trenton area. Cadwalader was to cross the Delaware at Bristol with men from Pennsylvania and New England and march on Bordentown. A second division of 1,000 men from Pennsylvania and New Jersey was to cross the river opposite Trenton and seize the bridge over the Assunpink, thus cutting off Rall's retreat. Finally, Washington himself with 2,400 men and eighteen cannon would lead a direct assault on Trenton, crossing from McConkey's Ferry and marching down to Trenton. If perfect timing could be achieved, the Hessian garrison could be cut off and annihilated.

Luckily for Washington and the American cause, Rall had completely disregarded his orders to fortify his position. A mixture of contempt and drunkenness left the Germans with no trenches or redoubts and a commander who spent his nights gambling and drinking. Angry at their treatment by the British, citizens from Hopewell flocked down to the Delaware River to help the American forces unload their supplies from the boats as sleet pounded the area. The British Light Dragoons quickly fled upon encountering the enemy. The Hessians were taken by surprise, and Rall's orderly had to awaken him twice from his inebriated slumber.

Greene parked his cannon at the intersection of King and Queen Streets, while Washington's troops moved through the city pushing the Hessians before them. Rall was mortally wounded, and the Germans

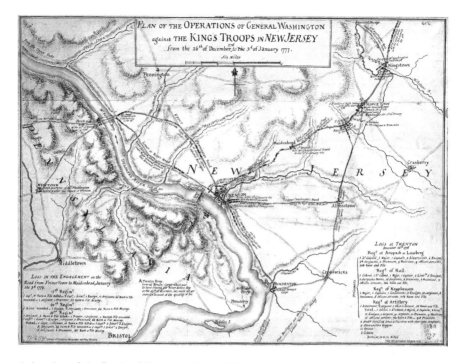

A drawing of the Battle of Trenton. *Library of Congress.*

began to quickly surrender. In less than two hours, the battle was over. The Americans would report only four soldiers wounded, including future president James Monroe. In exchange, they would net eight hundred Hessian prisoners, one thousand muskets, six cannon and forty horses. The sheer number of prisoners to be looked after, and the worsening conditions on the river, prompted Washington to withdraw back to Pennsylvania. In fact, the retreat proved to be more costly than the battle, with two-fifths of the men reported as unfit for duty the next day in camp.

Washington's feat rankled the British command. With American patrols reaching as far as Princeton, outlying English and Hessian units were quickly withdrawn to that town. By New Year's Day, Cornwallis was on his way back from New York City with plans to proceed against Washington in Trenton; the British were intent on holding on to New Jersey. Relying on his own fortune to pay his men, Washington managed to piece together an army of around 5,200. While working to fortify the eastern bank of the Assunpink, the Americans dispatched a sizeable force up the Princeton road toward Cornwallis. This unit, combined with the muddy conditions of the ground, served to delay the English and buy time for the Continentals. It would take Cornwallis ten hours to march the ten miles to Trenton, and after four assaults, he failed to dislodge the stubborn rebel army. The British settled in for the night, confident that Washington was trapped and that victory was certain the next day. With the rising of the sun, they discovered to their horror that despite the sounds of digging all night and the presence of thousands of campfires, the Americans had secretly withdrawn, safely extricating their army along some little-known routes, and were marching on Princeton. The Second Battle of Trenton again showed Washington's unique ability to command and elude.

Proceeding up Sand Town Road (modern-day Hamilton Avenue), the American army moved northeast over the Barrens, past Bear Swamp and up Quaker Road toward Princeton. A sharp drop in temperature froze the muddy roads over, allowing for quicker movement on the part of the rebels. Mercer's brigade, which was sent to delay the British by destroying the bridge over the Stony Brook River, was soon set upon by the British under Charles Mawhood. His tired troops began to give way, and Mercer himself was unhorsed and bayoneted seven times. Panic quickly spread, with Greene's Pennsylvania troops falling back as well. Only the determined fire of Moulder's battery and the arrival of Washington saved the day for the American army.

Washington quickly rallied the Continental soldiers, pushing Mawhood back and killing or wounding a quarter of the British force. "It's a fine fox chase, my boys," exclaimed Washington as his men advanced deeper into Princeton. One of the first cannonballs fired by Alexander Hamilton's battery punctured Nassau Hall, tearing through a portrait of George II.[62] Approximately three hundred English soldiers were eventually captured, compared to a loss of only thirty-four Americans. Mercer succumbed to his wounds nine days later, eventually giving his name to the county in which he fell.

The American force slowly withdrew toward the north. Destroying the bridge at Kingston, Washington stayed at Somerset Court House (Millstone) before eventually moving on to Pluckemin. By January 6, 1777, he was in Morristown, finally settling down for the winter, while Cornwallis withdrew to New Brunswick. At the same time, militiamen finished clearing out Hackensack, Newark and Elizabethtown. In a matter of weeks, Washington had transformed the situation on the

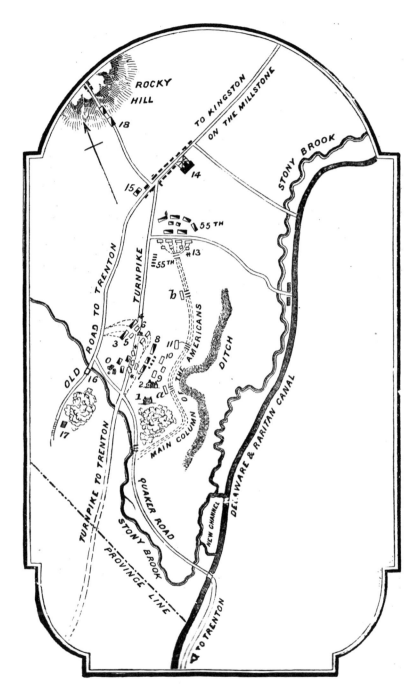

The movement of troops during the Battle of Princeton. *From Benson John Lossing's* Field Book of the Revolution *(1850).*

General Washington at the Battle of Monmouth. *National Archives.*

ground in New Jersey, reducing the British foothold to a narrow zone around Staten Island.

The Forage War that followed would last until early spring and, when combined with the previous actions at Trenton and Princeton, would produce more casualties for the British than the New York Campaign. Springfield, Chatham, Connecticut Farms, Bonhamtown, Millstone, Woodbridge, Spanktown and Drake's Farm all became the sites of skirmishes between the two armies as the winter wore on. Camp life, though, proved to be anything but easy for the soldiers, as lack of pay, scarcity of food and the ravages of disease took their toll. A company of artillerymen at Princeton deserted once their rum rations ran out, while many more turned over their arms to the British army for a promised twenty dollars. Washington took the unprecedented step of vaccinating his army at Morristown, something unheard of at the time, to help combat outbreaks of smallpox and reduce his casualties. The English were not immune either, with episodes of the disease erupting in Perth Amboy and New Brunswick and desertions spreading through the garrisons.

The spring of 1777 saw the British returning to the offensive in New Jersey. An assault by Cornwallis on Bound Brook in mid-April resulted in the capture of one hundred sheep and cows but little else. A massive operation toward the same location by Howe in June ground to a halt due to guerrilla warfare and Washington's refusal to commit to battle. A similar attempt against Lord Stirling at Short Hills likewise produced little result. By July, the English commander was beginning to evacuate the state and ferry his troops to Staten Island. Washington celebrated the first Fourth of July at Middlebrook and could boast control over all of New Jersey except for Paulus Hook for the first time since before the invasion of New York. Ignoring his assigned orders for a grand campaign against New York State, Howe then proceeded to sail south around Cape May for Philadelphia. Despite a campaign of misinformation, by August 24, Washington himself was in Philadelphia organizing a defense of the city. Yet within four weeks, following a series of defeats, the capital of the new nation had fallen.

The only barriers to further English expansion in the region were the various forts constructed on the New Jersey side of the Delaware River. Prominent among these was the fort built at Billingsport. Purchased by Congress on July 5, 1776, for £600, it was perhaps the first land purchase of the new country. Located at present-day Paulsboro, it protected a vast *cheval-de-frise* of iron-tipped wooden timbers in the river. This fortification was complemented further upriver by Fort Mifflin on Great Mud Island and Fort Mercer at Red Bank. Billingsport proved early to be indefensible and was abandoned, while a British assault on Mifflin by Von Donop resulted in four hundred Hessian casualties, including the colonel himself.[63] Subsequent attempts by the British navy to bombard the fort led to the destruction of the HMS *Augusta* and *Merlin*. It would take many more weeks of slow bombardment and another tenacious defense of Mifflin before both structures were finally abandoned. By December 18, Washington withdrew his army to Valley Forge for the winter, while Howe hunkered down in Philadelphia. Again the fortitude of the American army in New Jersey had halted the English juggernaut.

The spring of 1778 saw a return to the Forage War that had characterized operations in 1777. General "Mad" Anthony Wayne marched through southwestern New Jersey to gather up supplies and deny them to the British in a modern-day *chevauchée*. An English raid launched in response in March under Mawhood resulted in little substantial gain. British regulars and the Queen's Rangers engaged a party of militia at Quinton's Bridge over the Alloway Creek, eventually pushing them back. The Hancock House Massacre that followed would lead to the death of over twenty men, by far the vast majority of casualties from the operation.

The eventual evacuation of the British from Philadelphia had more to do with the nascent French alliance than the generalship of Washington. Ordered to retreat to New York City overland through New Jersey, General Clinton began his slow march through the state in mid-June. In an attempt to delay the British pending the arrival of the French fleet, Washington set off in pursuit of the English army. General Lee was dispatched on June 28 amid one-hundred-degree temperatures to halt the rear guard under Cornwallis at Monmouth. His poor leadership resulted in a rout of the Continental forces, and only the arrival and strong leadership of Washington again averted disaster. By the next day, the Americans held the battlefield, but Cornwallis was able to continue his march to Sandy Hook. The largest battle of the Revolution was over, having produced little for either side other than the court-martial of Charles Lee at Englishtown and the legend of Molly Pitcher.

As the war ground to a halt in the North, the Americans and British eyed one another while camped around occupied New York City. With the sole remaining British possession in New Jersey being Paulus Hook in modern-day Jersey City, it was only a matter of time before it became the target of a Patriot attack. Inspired by Anthony Wayne's raid on Stony Point, Major Henry Lee III proposed his own attack on Paulus Hook. On August 19, 1779, Lee with over 300 men quickly gained control of the fort, killing or wounding 50 men and capturing 158, all for the loss of only 2 men. For this momentous achievement, Congress granted a medal of bravery to Lee, the only non-general to receive such an award during the war.

The English likewise launched their own raids and sorties from Manhattan against both New Jersey and New York. One of the largest occurred in June 1780 when Lieutenant General Wilhem von Kynphausen sailed from Staten Island to Elizabethtown with six thousand English, Hessians and New Jersey Loyalists. Having received intelligence that Washington's army was crippled due to desertion and disease, the British planned to march toward Hobart Gap and gain access through the Watchung Mountains. The operation proved in the end to be a disaster. Stiff resistance by local militia at Connecticut Farms in modern-day Union combined with the timely arrival of Washington to convince Von Kynphausen to withdraw.

A few weeks later, the British launched a second assault to gain Hobart Gap, resulting in the Battle of Springfield. Nathanael Greene organized both Continentals and militia to halt the advance and, despite the burning

Springfield Presbyterian Church, where James Caldwell preached. *Courtesy of Daniel Case.*

of Springfield, ultimately managed to do so. The battle also saw the heroic action of Reverend James Caldwell, whose wife had been killed by the British a few weeks before at Connecticut Farms. Seeing the artillerymen run short on wadding, Caldwell distributed hymn books to the soldiers, famously saying, "Give 'em Watts, boys." The most notable casualty of the battle was former Speaker of the assembly Stephen Crane, who the British barbarously bayoneted while marching to Springfield.

An American unit under General Wayne would launch its own raid a month later. Aimed at reducing a Loyalist blockhouse at Bull's Ferry, the attack ended in failure. Yet "Light Horse" Harry Lee did manage to drive off most of the cattle being kept in the area for the British army. Major Andre, of Benedict Arnold fame, memorialized the battle in a poem entitled "Cow Chase" that was published in the *Royal Gazette*. Finally, two British raids launched the next year in 1780 assaulted both Newark and Hackensack. The latter town saw its courthouse and jail burned to the ground by the king's forces.

Yet not all the New Jersey soldiers remained as devoted to the cause once rations and pay ran low and the hardships of war carried into its sixth year. On January 20, 1781, hundreds of soldiers of the regiments camped near Bloomingdale mutinied. Following the example of Pennsylvania soldiers who had undertaken a similar action only weeks before, the men began to march on the state capital to demand better conditions and back pay. Though General Wayne had used troops from New Jersey to successfully diffuse the Pennsylvania mutiny, those same men were now partaking in an uprising of their own.

General Washington wrote to General Robert Howe at West Point, ordering him to suppress the rebellion, forcing them to accept "unconditional submission, and I am to desire you will grant no terms while they are with arms in their hands in a state of resistance…If you succeed in compelling the revolted troops to a surrender you will instantly execute a few of the most active and most incendiary leaders."[64] On January 27, Howe successfully put down the mutiny. Two of the officers, Sergeants David Gilmore and John Tuttle, were executed by a firing squad composed of their own men. In the end, through this violent repression, the threat of mutiny was quelled.

NONMILITARY CONTRIBUTIONS

New Jersey's industry rallied early on to support the war effort. For example, though the state had no major saltworks before the war, by the Revolution's end, upward of twenty had been constructed along the coast. The importance of salt was plainly clear to both Congress, which promoted the construction of these works, and the British in New York. Taking note of the various saltworks along the Jersey shore, the English launched a raid against the one in Toms River in 1782. Carrying the blockhouse, they captured the garrison and reduced the saltworks to ashes. Following the fight, New Jersey Loyalists under Richard Lippincott took Captain Joshua Huddy from Toms River to the Atlantic Highlands, where he was hanged. This atrocity led to the Asgill Affair, one of the first major diplomatic tests of the new nation.

Perhaps New Jersey's greater material contribution to the war effort was in the form of gunpowder. Most of the black powder in the colonies at the start of the Revolution was surplus from the French and Indian War. To hamper the efforts of the colonists, the British had outlawed shipments of gunpowder to America as early as October 1774. Thus, in April 1776, Colonel Jacob Ford Jr. began the construction of a mill in Morristown, the only mill in New Jersey at the time, to produce powder for Washington's army. Petitioning the New Jersey Committee of Safety for funding, he was granted £2,000 interest free for a year. Though he died from disease in 1777, Ford's mansion became the headquarters of Washington from 1779 to 1780 while he wintered in the Morristown area. Yet not all Patriots were as successful as Ford. Adonijah Peacock of Medford likewise produced powder for the American army. Unfortunately for him, while drying some powder, he was killed after an accidental explosion.

Where battles and industry ended, the contributions of individuals in New Jersey began as the state produced numerous commanders of note. Alexander of Basking Ridge, better known as Lord Stirling, was notable for his actions and bravery at Brooklyn Heights, Brandywine and Germantown. David Forman, known as "Devil David," was quite effective as a militia commander in helping to break up Tory formations and plots within the state. William Maxwell of Warren County, who had previously fought in the French and Indian War, served as an officer in most of the major campaigns from Canada to Philadelphia. In addition to the generals provided by the state, thousands of individual soldiers enlisted as well. Some of the more famous of them were Joseph Bloomfield; Aaron Burr; the Quaker Thomas Carpenter, who served as paymaster for the New Jersey militia; future congressman Jonathan Dayton, who was implicated in Burr's conspiracy; John Doughty, who was senior officer of the army in 1784; John Mott; Aaron Ogden, who became the fifth governor of the state and achieved even more fame in the monumental Supreme Court case of *Gibbons v. Ogden*; future governor William Pennington; and John Stevens, who built the first steam ferry and locomotive in the nation and whose son helped finance the Stevens Institute of Technology.

One of the more notorious New Jersey participants in the war was Matthias Ogden. Captured in November 1780 and later released as part of a prisoner exchange, Ogden developed a rather ambitious plan. In September 1781, he began to formulate an operation to kidnap the crown prince, William Henry. Then stationed in New York City with Admiral Robert Digby, the seventeen-year-old prince presented a tantalizing target for the Patriots. George Washington was well aware of the plot, writing in March 1782 to Ogden that "the spirit of enterprise so conspicuous in your plan for surprising in their quarters, & bringing off the Prince-William Henry & Admiral Digby, merits applause; and you have my authority to make the attempt in any manner, & at such a time as your own judgment shall direct."[65] In the end, the operation was called off, but it showed the levels to which creative and dedicated residents of New Jersey would go to bring the war to a close.

Other notable citizens include John Honeyman and Patience Lovell Wright. The former was a legendary spy who, according to many traditional accounts, not only kept Washington informed of the strength of the Hessians at Trenton but also lulled the Germans in general—and Rall in particular—into a false sense of security. Patience Wright, who is alleged to have been America's first sculptor, is storied to have been a spy during the war. While in England, she secreted information to Congress inside the wax heads she molded.

In the end, the contributions of New Jersey to the war for American independence were as varied as those of its citizens. The coastline of the province provided opportunity for trade, privateering and large ship-to-ship battles. The fields of the state produced food for the armies, materials for combat and animals for transportation and sustenance. Its geography led to the region's becoming the pivot point of the Revolution, providing the apex and nadir of the war. Finally, the people of the state contributed their fortunes, lives and intelligence toward defeating the British and achieving liberty. Though the war did not start or end in New Jersey, it can be said without too much patriotic hyperbole that it was won there.

CHAPTER 4

FROM LITTLE TURTLE TO TECUMSEH: NEW JERSEY AND THE WARS OF THE EARLY REPUBLIC

The Constitution had barely been ratified before the men of New Jersey were again called on to defend the nation. Rather than a period of republican peace and virtue, the first twenty years of the new nation saw a series of Indian wars out west, armed rebellions close to home and an undeclared war against France. All of these conflicts would again see the citizens of the state rally to the flag to protect the land and shores of New Jersey, and those of the larger country.

NEW JERSEY'S WARS IN THE NORTHWEST

The first post-Revolutionary conflict to involve the United States was the Northwest Indian War. Spanning a decade, this often-forgotten campaign against a massive confederation of Native Americans was fought over control of the vast Ohio region. Questions over ownership of the area were still unanswered following both the French and Indian War and American Revolution. Raids and counter-raids between the natives of the Western Confederacy and the American settlers of the region began in earnest in 1785. A report from Major John Doughty of New Jersey, former senior officer of the army, to Secretary of War Henry Knox early on in the conflict expressed Doughty's opinion that the British were helping to foment trouble between the Indians and Americans, including selling arms and encouraging attacks.[66] By October 1787, Congress requested an army of 700 men to protect the western frontier. These men were to be drawn from four states, with New Jersey responsible for the raising of 110 men.

In the fall of 1789, Doughty built Fort Washington at modern-day Cincinnati to protect settlers in the region. By December, he received orders from General Josiah Harmar stating that President Washington wished him to travel south to establish a fort at Muscle Shoals in Alabama and negotiate with the Choctaw tribes along the way. Harmar specifically suggested to Doughty that "if the post be established with an adequate force, it will enable us either to intimidate the Creeks or to strike them with success."[67] Doughty dutifully traveled to the mouth of the Tennessee bearing a letter from the president introducing both him and his mission:

> *I have sent Major Doughty, one of our Warriors, in order to convince you that the United States well remember the treaty they made with your Nation…guard and protect him…Be attentive to what he shall say in the name of the United States for he will speak only truth.*[68]

Hearing of Doughty's movements, a Cree chief named Alexander McGillivray dispatched a war party of Cree, Shawnee, Cherokee and Chickamauga. About two hundred miles up the Tennessee River, the officer from New Jersey and his small band of sixteen men were decimated by the Indians. With six men killed and five grievously wounded, Doughty retreated to the Spanish fort at New Madrid, a settlement founded by fellow New Jersey resident Colonel George Morgan, who had intended to found a buffer state between America and Spanish America.

The war continued for another five years. Following Harmar's disastrous campaign of 1790, Secretary of War Knox proposed the raising of additional levies to support a new offensive in the region. For its part in this endeavor, New Jersey raised one battalion of men in the spring of 1791 under Major Thomas Patterson. By the fall, these men, as part of the Second Regiment of Levies, were marching from New Brunswick to Pittsburgh to join the army then being assembled under General Arthur St. Clair. Poorly equipped, badly trained and departing late in the season, the assembled force was massacred at the Battle of the Wabash on November 4. With over 97 percent of the soldiers engaged killed or wounded, the battle represents the worst defeat ever in American military history. As the New Jersey battalion had been stationed to the right, it escaped relatively unscathed when compared to the vast majority of other units in St. Clair's army. Among those New Jersey militiamen who were engaged in the battle and who managed to escape was Captain Zebulon Pike of Woodbridge, father of the famed explorer.

President Washington, under intense pressure from Congress, raised the first national, professional army since the end of the Revolution. Among its ranks were many men from New Jersey, including some of those who had fought with St. Clair at Wabash. After months of intense training, the Legion of the United States under General "Mad" Anthony Wayne met the Native Confederation at the Battle of Fallen Timbers. Following its complete victory, the United States established peace with the Indians, acquiring large tracts of territory in the region.

Rebellions and Insurgencies

The 1790s saw the onset of two rebellions in the state of Pennsylvania. Following so closely behind Shay's Rebellion, which helped to bring down the government under the Articles of Confederation, the new government took both incidents seriously. The Whiskey Rebellion and Fries's Rebellion both erupted over the issue of taxation, which many of the rural residents of Pennsylvania felt was unduly placed on them. The proactive response of Congress to both occurrences would lean heavily on the states for men and supplies. Due to its proximity to the conflict, New Jersey would be one of the first states called on to aid in its suppression.

The Whiskey Rebellion erupted with a vengeance in 1794. By May of that year, Congress, under Speaker of the House Jonathan Dayton of New Jersey, issued a call for troops from the surrounding states. President Washington requested that Governor Richard Howell dispatch the New Jersey militia to Pennsylvania. On September 17, Brigadier General Anthony Walton White crossed the Delaware River with the New Jersey cavalry, while the governor, as commander-in-chief, followed with the infantry five days later. Writing to his mother, Howell expressed his view that "it would ill become an old soldier to sit calmly by and see the ruin of his country; and on that principle I take an active part."[69]

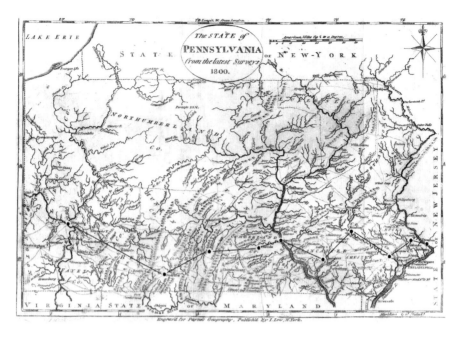

The path of Governor Howell's march through Pennsylvania to confront the Whiskey rebels. *Author's collection.*

Howell marched his men from Trenton toward the western regions of Pennsylvania. Passing through Newtown, Norristown, Reading, Hummelstown and Swatara, they reached Harrisburg by October 3. Joined by their commander-in-chief along with additional units, the army left Carlisle for Shippingsburg, Strasburg, Blue Mountain, Horse Valley, Cattertona Mountain, Path Valley and Tuscarora. From October 17 to October 23, the army camped at New Bedford. However, the rain of late fall led to muddy conditions that slowed down movement considerably. It wouldn't be until November 15 that the army approached its final destination of Pittsburgh.

Yet the show of force by Washington worked. The various bands of rebels began to disperse, and the insurrection was declared over. By November 20, the troops from New Jersey were already departing for home. Toward the end of the campaign, however, grievances because of the weather as well as dissatisfaction over the prospect of having to shoot at fellow Americans led to rumblings of mutiny among the New Jersey soldiers. To help raise morale and distract his men, Governor Howell wrote and popularized a tune that his men quickly adopted.

The song, "Jersey Blues," would continue to be a favorite of soldiers from the state for years.

To arms once more our hero cries
Sedition lives and order dies,
To peace and ease then bid adieu
And dash to the mountains, Jersey Blue.

Chorus:
Dash to the mountains, Jersey Blue,
Jersey Blue,
Jersey Blue,
And dash to the mountains, Jersey Blue.

Since proud ambition rears its head
And murders, rage, and discord spread,
To save from spoil the virtuous few
Dash over the mountains, Jersey Blue.

Rous'd at the call, with magic sound,
The drum and trumpets circle round,
As soon the crops their routes pursue,
So dash to the mountains, Jersey Blue.

Unstain'd with crimes, unus'd to fear,
In deep array our youths appear
And fly to crush the rebel crew
Or die in the mountains, Jersey Blue.

Tho' tears bedew the maidens cheek,
And storm hangs round the mountains bleak,
'Tis glory calls, to love adieu,
Then dash to the mountains, Jersey Blue.

Should foul misrule and party rage
With law and liberty engage,
Push home your steel, you'll soon review
Your native plains, brave Jersey Blue.[70]

The outbreak of Fries's Rebellion in 1799 followed a similar storyline. Complaints over the raising of taxes to pay for the Quasi War erupted among German settlers in southeastern Pennsylvania. President Adams responded in the same vigorous way as had Washington. Federal troops were called out to the region, and requests were sent out to Pennsylvania and New Jersey to call up their militias. Governor Howell agreed to ready two thousand militiamen and cavalry, much as he had during the Whiskey Rebellion. In the end, the minor rebellion was put down even quicker than the previous tax revolt. The New Jersey soldiers soon dispersed, and President Adams eventually pardoned all those involved.

THE QUASI WAR

As the French Revolution spilled over its borders and dragged in the rest of Europe, it was only a matter of time before its ripples were felt in America. Fear of a French invasion, the marauding of French privateers off the coast of the United States, the depredations of the Reign of Terror, the XYZ Affair and concerns over French émigrés and their political influence prompted a response from Congress and President Adams. The Quasi War raged between the United States and France from 1798 to 1800, and New Jersey was again actively involved in the conflict in multiple areas.

As a purely naval war, the coastline and ports of New Jersey experienced the full effect of the Quasi War. Captain Thomas Truxtun, commander of the USS *Constellation* and resident of Perth Amboy, recommended that city as early as February 1798 to Secretary of War McHenry for a potential port out of which the navy could operate. In the end, the secretary decided against the move, but privateers and merchantmen still sailed from the Raritan Bay throughout the conflict. Five months later, the waters of New Jersey in fact witnessed the first major American victory of the war. The USS *Delaware* was patrolling off Egg Harbor when it encountered a ransacked merchant vessel. Captain Stephen Decatur had begun to search for the responsible French warship when he spotted four boats on the horizon. To ensure that the French would not flee, he pretended to run, drawing the *La Croyable* after him. The twelve guns of the French ship proved to be no match for the twenty of the *Delaware*. Decatur captured the warship and secured America's first victory in the campaign. Ironically, it was also a resident from New Jersey aboard the captured and renamed *La Croyable* who cost the nation its first loss. Lieutenant William Bainbridge of Princeton, while commanding the renamed USS *Retaliation*, was taken by two French privateers in the West Indies.

Additional naval commanders from the state included Charles Stewart and Thomas Tingey. Stewart, while commanding the USS *Experiment* with the West Indies Squadron, captured the French ships *Deux Amis*, *La Diana* and *Louisa Bridger* between September and December 1800. Captain Tingey commanded the USS *Ganges* and, in 1799, captured numerous American ships that were illegally trading with the French, as well as the French ships *Le Vanqueur*, *La Rabateuse*, *L'Eugene* and *L'Esperance*.

Though a French invasion never took place, the Federalist Party had reason to fear it could and sought to prepare the nation for that possibility. Alexander Hamilton was the strongest voice behind building up the military in preparations for a war with France and to enable his own rise to power. Thus, it came as no surprise when he was named major general of the army, in charge of handling the day-to-day affairs for the aged General Washington. Various New Jersey politicians and officers were given high positions in the new army as well. These included Senator Jonathan Dayton, who was named a brigadier general, and Major John Doughty, who was made an officer in the artillery. Dayton would eventually turn down the commission in order to remain in Congress, though his brother did become heavily involved with contracts to supply the soldiers stationed in New Jersey.

The Quasi War, however, produced a partisan split within the state assembly not seen since the various French and Indian wars. Pro-French/anti-Hamilton Republicans early on began to oppose the actions of the president and Governor Howell. At the start of the invasion scare in 1798, Republican militia officers in the state refused to sign up for service, calling Adams a tyrant and arguing that he had violated the Constitution. Governor Howell, furious at this display of disloyalty, referred to the Republicans in the state as "shreds of a French faction [that operated as a] dagger in the hands of…[a French] assassin."[71] In fact, political allegiance rather than military pedigree was quickly becoming the determining factor in the state for the selection of officers. On November 19, Secretary McHenry wrote to Senator Dayton requesting a list of potential soldiers, exempting those who were "indisposed to government and order."[72] It was in this vein in March 1799 that Dayton wrote to Hamilton recommending Major Ford of Morris County as a good Federalist among a "torrent of Jacobinism more prevalent there than in any quarter of the state."[73]

Governor Howell would eventually raise three regiments of soldiers. During the course of the war, they would remain stationed in Perth Amboy, preparing for a conflict that was never to come. The war ended with the Convention of 1800, permanently dissolving the Franco-American alliance. The Federalists were damaged as a national brand, losing the White House in 1800 to Jefferson and the Republicans. Likewise, Howell's battles with the legislature in New Jersey helped secure the governor's chair for Joseph Bloomfield in 1801. As the new governor himself wrote to President Jefferson, "The same spirit which has lately pervaded the union and changed the Administration of the general government has had its proportionate effects in the State of New-Jersey."[74]

THE TRIPOLITAN WAR

The ascension of the Republicans to power under Jefferson saw various changes in domestic and foreign policy. One of the earliest examples of this was the president's abandonment of the previous two administrations' policy of paying tribute to the Barbary States of North Africa, which then led the country into its next war. In fact, the last American ship to sail into the harbor of Algiers with the annual tribute payment was the USS *George Washington* under the command of Princeton resident William Bainbridge.

Bainbridge would return to North Africa three years later aboard the USS *Philadelphia*. Under orders to blockade Tripoli, the American ship sailed into the harbor ready to confront the privateer ships docked there. Unfortunately, the warship struck an uncharted reef on October 23, 1803, and became stuck. Despite Bainbridge's valiant efforts to refloat it, the ship and its crew were captured by the Barbary pirates. The crew was held for nineteen months before being rescued by an American force.

Another native of New Jersey, Richard Somers from Great Egg Harbor, was in command of the USS *Nautilus* as it sailed for North Africa. Between August 3 and September 3, 1804, Somers participated in five attacks on Tripoli. On September 4, he was placed in command of the fire ship *Intrepid*, which had been fitted out to explode in the harbor, causing massive damage to the gathered pirate vessels. Somers and his volunteer crew sailed into the harbor, coming under fire from the batteries along the shore. Thirty minutes after the operation began and before the ship got to its final position, the *Intrepid* exploded. Somers and his crew of twelve were instantly killed as the ship was torn apart. Their bodies were eventually buried in a mass grave after washing up on shore and being subjected to defilement by the residents of the city. Though the New Jersey Assembly passed a resolution in 2004 hoping to have the remains of Bainbridge returned, with the nation's Congress following suit in 2011 after the uprising against Muammar Gaddafi, no action has yet been taken. At the end of the war, the United States Congress honored additional various men for gallantry, including numerous residents of New Jersey, most notably Joseph Bainbridge, William M. Crane, James Lawrence, Charles Stewart and Edward Trenchard.

The War of 1812

What was sometimes termed the Second War for Independence was fought much farther afield from New Jersey than was the first. No major battles erupted on its soil, it was never occupied by the enemy and its population was largely left untouched by the ravages of war. Yet the contributions of the Garden State to the War of 1812 were considerable and occurred in almost as many fields as its contribution to the American Revolution.

Unresolved issues with the United Kingdom, some stretching back to the Revolution, pushed the two countries closer and closer to war during the first decade of the nineteenth century. Impressment, one of the largest issues, personally impacted the sailing state of New Jersey. Numerous sailors from the state plied the ocean in vessels that were periodically stopped, searched and even seized by the English. In May 1811, the British warship HMS *Guerriere* stopped the USS *Spitfire*, a warship, off the coast of Sandy Hook, seizing an American sailor from that vessel in a virtual repeat of the famed Chesapeake-Leopard Affair of 1807.

Public opinion in the seafaring state was quickly aroused by such actions. As early as 1807, in response to the Chesapeake Affair, the city of Newark had written to President Jefferson requesting war and promising to form a committee of correspondence:

> *That although this meeting greatly deprecates the calamity of war, yet should this become necessary for the preservation of the personal rights of their fellow citizens, the defence [sic] of the country, and the maintenance of the sovereignty and independence of the Union, they will engage in it with alacrity, and solemnly pledge to our country and our government, our lives and fortunes in defence [sic] of the rights of an independent nation.*[75]

In January 1812, Samuel Pennington of Essex County introduced similar legislation into the state assembly:

> *That in case the government of the United States shall eventually determine to resist by force the lawless aggressions committed by the British nation on the persons and property of our citizens, this Legislature, in behalf of themselves and the citizens of New Jersey, whose representatives they are, pledge themselves to the nation to render to the general government all the aid, assistance and support in their power, and will, with all readiness, perform all the duties required of them in the prosecution of a war undertaken for the common defense and general welfare.*

In fact, preparations began months before the formal declaration of war. In 1812, New Jersey had thirty-five thousand men eligible for military service. In April, the state's quota for a potential war with England was placed at five thousand men, who, according to Adjutant General James J. Wilson, "by prompt obedience to this requisition, and by conduct and bravery in the field, should there be an occasion to take it, the militia of New Jersey will sustain the character they acquired during the Revolutionary War, while they assert the rights of our insulted country, maintain the independence of the nation, and support the government of their choice."[76] The following month, President Madison appointed Governor Joseph Bloomfield as a brigadier general of the Third Military District headquartered in New York City.

Yet in a similar vein to the Quasi War, which had split the state between the Federalists and the Republicans, the conflict proved to be anything but universally popular among citizens of New Jersey. When Congress did vote on a declaration of war in June, every congressman from the state voted against the measure despite the fact that they were all members of President's Madison's party. The close vote in Congress—79 to 49 in the House and 19 to 13 in the Senate—reveals both the unpopularity of the decision and the fractured interest of the United States at the time. Nowhere was this truer than New Jersey, where despite its Republican-dominated legislature, executive and national representation, the strong Quaker, industrial and mercantile interests in the state disapproved of the decision to go to war. In fact, in elections for that year following the declaration of war, the Federalist Party swept back into power in the state. Both houses of the state legislature were carried with the acquisition of three Republican-controlled counties, thanks to a coalition of merchants, Quakers and West Jersey interests. In national politics, voters in the state sent four Federalists and two Republicans to the House of Representatives for the Thirteenth Congress, where previously they had sat all Republicans since 1801. In the presidential election of that year, electors from New Jersey chose Federalist anti-war candidate DeWitt Clinton, again despite having voted Republican since 1804.

Thanks to the switch in power in the state legislature, Federalist Aaron Ogden was named governor in 1812. Though he advertised an anti-war agenda, once in the executive's chair, he had to deal with the realities of the situation. Ogden quickly sought $5,000 from the assembly for war expenses. In response, the Federalist-dominated body passed a resolution condemning the war as "inexpedient, ill-timed, and most dangerous impolitic."[77] Yet as they were unable to stop the conflict, they resorted to simply obstructing the process—working to protect the state but opposed to the aims of Madison in Canada. For example, the legislature passed a series of bills outlawing the use of the militia to defend either New York City or Philadelphia. Unfortunately, their efforts failed to find support among the populace, and the Republicans again secured control of the state in 1813. Though President Madison offered to make Ogden a major general, he turned down the offer, continuing to work for the party within New Jersey.

Only two days after war was declared, Governor Bloomfield ordered eleven companies of militia to gather at Paulus Hook for a "camp of instruction" under Major Isaac Andruss. As was mentioned, Bloomfield himself was made a general by President Madison and soon after proceeded with eight thousand men to a base at Plattsburgh, where he began to train them. Bloomfield's contributions to the war were recognized by both his enemies and allies in New Jersey, and he was toasted in July at a Republican meeting: "When in the camp, on the march, or under the walls of Quebec, may he never want the genuine character of a Jersey Blue."[78] Ogden continued to call out more militiamen in November 1812, and by the end of the year, Jersey Blues were stationed at Fort Richmond on Staten Island as well as on the Atlantic Highlands.

The industries of New Jersey again rose to the challenge of supplying the armies in the field. Batsto Village, which had played such an important role during the American Revolution in supplying iron and cannonballs to Washington's army, again worked to meet the demands of war. The iron foundries located there would reach the height of their production capabilities from the War of 1812 through the 1820s. The scarcities caused by the British blockade only increased the industrial spirit and ingenuity of the residents of New Jersey, especially at places such as the bog iron foundries of Allaire Village and the furnaces at Mount Hope and Hibernia. Additionally, Paterson, as the model industrial city of the state, saw its factories in demand for the production of war materials. Henry Clay Mill, which opened in that city in 1811, almost immediately began producing uniforms for the men in the field. Overall, the small but thriving town grew tremendously during the war but experienced an economic downturn following the establishment of peace. Newark followed suit, with one businessman, Robert B. Campfield, who made a small fortune off war contracts showing his patriotism by commissioning fourteen cannon outside of his place of business on Broad Street, one for each county in the state.[79] In the end, the Industrial Revolution, which swept the state and the nation following the Treaty of Ghent, can in part be attributed to the war itself. New Jersey's transformation into an industrial state was catalyzed by the war.

Though the soil of New Jersey did not witness any battles during the war, its coastline was the scene of numerous engagements. On July 17, only three weeks after the declaration of war, the first loss of a ship by either side took place off the coast of northern New Jersey. The USS *Nautilus*, which was under the command of William M. Crane of Elizabethtown, was captured by the HMS *Shannon*. The latter had been patrolling the coast off New Jersey as part of a five-ship squadron. Additional British units arrived over the course of the war, tightening the blockade of the nation. Numerous raids took place along the Jersey shore from Sandy Hook to Cumberland County in 1813 and 1814, especially in the area of Barnegat Inlet. Commodore Thomas Hardy of the HMS *Ramillies* famously conducted raids around the inlet, most notably in March 1813, when two vessels were burned and a landing party killed fifteen head of cattle. So successful were the actions of Hardy along the coast that the state instituted a draft of men along the shore to defend the region. One in every seven men was chosen, with most being sent to Sandy Hook, much as during the Revolution.[80] General Abraham Godwin of Paterson personally marched a group of volunteers to the shore to dig trenches and other fortifications. Forts of stone and sand were constructed by militia up and down the Atlantic seaboard, including Somers Point, commanding the entrance to Great Egg Harbor, and Fort Gates on Sandy Hook.

Major ship battles also raged in the Atlantic Ocean off the coast of the state during the duration of the conflict. At the start of the war in July 1812, the USS *Constitution* was sailing north to join a squadron under John Rodgers. Approaching Egg Harbor, Captain Isaac Hull spotted the five British ships HMS *Aeolus*, *Africa*, *Belvidera*, *Guerriere* and *Shannon*. Though the wind failed, through the titanic effort of its crew, the *Constitution* was able to outrun the pursuing English fleet and make it safely to Boston.

One of the most famous naval actions of the war involved New Jersey resident James Lawrence. Given command of the USS *Hornet*, Lawrence captured the HMS *Peacock* off the Demerara River in South America on February 24, 1813. Promoted to the rank of captain, he was then placed in charge of the USS *Chesapeake* and sailed from Boston on May 31, 1813, to engage the HMS *Shannon*, which was stationed off the coast of Massachusetts. Seeking to avenge the disgrace that his ship had suffered from the HMS *Leopard* in 1807, Lawrence sought to engage the better-manned and trained British warship. In the confrontation that followed, the *Chesapeake* was heavily defeated by the *Shannon*, which was taken into the English navy after its crew was captured. Lawrence, who was shot by a sniper, became immortalized for his final words as he lay dying below deck: "Don't give up the ship." The phrase was to become sacred writ in the U.S. Navy.

On land, the state of New Jersey was represented in battle by the Fifteenth U.S. Infantry. Known as the New Jersey Regiment, the force was drafted almost entirely from the Garden State. It formed early in the war and was part of the force commanded by Major General Joseph Bloomfield at Sackett's Harbor, New York. Under the leadership of the famed explorer and veteran of the Battle of Tippecanoe, Colonel Zebulon Pike, the regiment trained for months. The men were uniformed in gray coats with black trim and, thanks to the innovative thought of their commander, were additionally armed with ten-foot pikes. Though largely unused since the early 1700s, Pike was convinced of the usefulness of the weapon. The November 28, 1812 *New York Spectator* reported:

> *Each subaltern is to carry a pike and a sword. The men are to form three deep—the tallest in the rear rank. The rear rank have lately had their gun barrels cut off about 12 inches, and not fitted for a bayonet. They are to be slung on the back, when they proceed to a charge. The rear rank are to carry a pike, somewhat of the form of a spontoon, attached to a pole 10 feet in length. Col. Pike thinks much of this kind of weapon, while others condemn them.*[81]

Eager to test the effectiveness of his men, Pike convinced his commanding officer to allow him to attempt a sortie across the Lacolle River. On a snowy night in November 1812, American units crossed the frozen stream to assault the British camp on the other side. Pike's carefully laid plans quickly fell apart as the Canadian units had withdrawn to the woods, leaving their empty huts and untended fires behind them. The two prongs of the invasion mistook each other in the dark for the enemy, and a deadly barrage of friendly fire erupted that left two dead and a handful wounded. After an exchange of five or six rounds, a semblance of order was restored, and Pike withdrew the New Jersey Regiment and the New York militia back over the river to the American camp. The soldiers rejoined the main army and proceeded to winter quarters at Plattsburgh.

The first major action of the Fifteenth came on April 27, 1813, with the assault on York in Ontario. The capital of Upper Canada, now known as Toronto, was a supply point and major port for the British in the region and thus represented a tempting target for the American army gathered at Sackett's Harbor. The first major amphibious attack of the war involved Colonel Pike leading the Fifteenth New Jersey along with various other regiments against the defenses of York. After a relatively quick engagement, the Americans drove back the British and Canadians and took the city. Unfortunately, the English rigged the town's magazine to explode, with the flying debris striking and killing Colonel Pike.

The New Jersey Regiment was next involved in the assault on Fort George. In May 1813, over four thousand American soldiers, including those from New Jersey, landed in waves against Fort George on the Niagara Peninsula. After the successful conquest of the important point overlooking the Niagara River, the Fifteenth Infantry garrisoned the fort during the tenure of its occupation. By December of that year, following a series of reversals suffered in Canada, the American army decided to withdraw from Fort George. The New Jersey Regiment was tasked with covering the retreat, and though it suffered heavy casualties in doing so, not one soldier from the state was captured by the enemy.

The final year of the war saw troops from New Jersey involved in a variety of other battles and campaigns. Included among these was the pivotal Battle of Plattsburgh, in which men from the Fifteenth under Captain McGlassin helped to defend Fort Brown from a British assault. A month later, members of the Fifteenth took part in one of the last actions in Canada as part of the attack on Cooks Mill. Yet in the end, this assault under Major General George Izard ultimately failed. The Americans abandoned and burned Fort Erie before withdrawing back over the border. As invasion fears mounted back home, artillery was placed on the various hills of Essex and Bergen County overlooking New York City, while a warning system of horsemen was organized to spread the alarm. In September 1814, over eight hundred volunteers from Newark marched to Brooklyn carrying flags, banners and signs reading "Don't Give Up the Soil" to help dig trenches and build fortifications in case of a British assault.[82]

Overall, the state contributed 5,668 men, 135 cavalry and 209 artillerymen to the war effort. General William Gould of Caldwell, who had fought in the Revolution, perhaps best sums up the demands on the men of New Jersey during this often-forgotten conflict with the orders he issued to the men of Essex County after the burning of Washington: "Soldiers! The eyes of the world are fixed on our Country; let us prove that we are worthy of our freedom; let every citizen become a Soldier, and every Soldier a Patriot." Although the War of 1812 gained no land for the nation nor famed battlefields for New Jersey, it nonetheless benefited both. America saw an end to impressment and a cessation of Indian attacks along the northern frontier and gained a new measure of respect abroad. New Jersey experienced a minor industrial boom that was to become the mainstay of its economic focus after the war. The state was a microcosm of the nation, and its economic transformation a mirror of what was to happen nationally over the next decade.

CHAPTER 5

FROM THE HALLS OF MONTEZUMA TO THE SHORES OF NEW JERSEY: NEW JERSEY AND MANIFEST DESTINY

As America expanded westward, so, too, did the population of New Jersey. Though the state did not claim or gain land from Manifest Destiny, various citizens and soldiers from the state were still involved in the process. This chapter will focus on a few specific residents, detailing their accomplishments toward this larger American victory and subsequent expansion.

Perhaps no name is more associated with Manifest Destiny or the military history of the nation during the first half of the nineteenth century than that of Winfield Scott. Though born in Virginia, the veteran of the War of 1812 married and settled in New Jersey in 1817. From that point until his death in 1866, "Old Fuss and Feathers" would serve in numerous wars and conflicts, longer than any other general to date, even becoming the first resident of the state to run for the office of president in 1852.

His first major command took place during the Black Hawk War, which raged in Illinois and Michigan in 1832. Upset by the lack of progress in the campaign, President Jackson appointed Scott to assume command in June. Unfortunately, his arrival was hampered and his troops decimated by an outbreak of cholera. Though the New Jersey officer would not arrive in time to see combat, another citizen of the state did. Joseph Throckmorton of Monmouth County designed and built the armed steamship *Warrior* in 1832. Pressed into service by the military, Throckmorton, with his ship, was sent to negotiate with the Sioux. While sailing the Mississippi River, the *Warrior* encountered Black Hawk's British Band attempting to cross the river. Throckmorton

The *Warrior* engaged at the Battle of Bad Axe in 1832. *Granger Collection.*

opened fire, killing twenty-three of the Indians and stopping the crossing. Though he had to break off the engagement to refuel, the *Warrior* was back in action the next day to participate in the Battle of Bad Axe, in which the militia under Atkinson combined with Throckmorton's steamship to kill or capture half of the native army, thus bringing an end to the war. Incidentally, the site of the battle was the same point at which New Jersey's own Zebulon Pike camped while on his voyage of exploration in 1805.

Scott later went on to serve in the Second Seminole War of 1836, the Creek War in the same year and the Aroostook War in 1839. In the first of these, he led an army into Florida in a failed attempt to bring the Seminole to battle. That same year, under orders from Jackson, Scott forcibly removed the remaining Creek Indians from Alabama to Indian Territory. Finally, his tactful diplomacy helped to diffuse the Aroostook War and peacefully settle the Maine-Canada boundary dispute. By 1841, Scott was made commanding general of the army, a post he was to hold for twenty years.

Another native of New Jersey, Lawrence Kearny of Perth Amboy, went on to play an important role in the U.S. Navy during the first half

Robert Stockton, the victor of California. *Library of Congress*.

of the nineteenth century. In 1818, Kearny took command of the USS *Enterprise* as part of the New Orleans Squadron. Thanks to his efforts, Jean Laffite, the famed pirate king of Louisiana who had once aided the Americans in the Battle of New Orleans, was permanently evicted from his base at Galveston, Texas. In 1842, while commanding the USS

Constellation, Lawrence helped to protect American interests in China during the Opium War. The following year, he was involved in diffusing the Paulet Affair, in which the British occupied the Kingdom of Hawaii for months before being peacefully evicted.

The culmination of Manifest Destiny was President Polk's acquisitions of Oregon and California. An entire generation had elapsed since New Jersey was engaged in a major war. Despite its Whig leanings, the state eagerly responded to the outbreak of hostilities. A desire to expand into the southwestern area of the continent had been present in the American psyche since the Louisiana Purchase. In fact, only a few years after that land acquisition, New Jersey's Zebulon Pike led an expedition through the region on the orders of General Wilkinson. Though on the surface the journey was ostensibly meant to explore the southeastern reaches of the Louisiana Purchase, it ended up being much more. Captured by Spanish forces and transported to Santa Fe, Pike made accurate observations of the defenses, geography and manpower of the region—information that was to prove invaluable during the Mexican War.

The declaration of war in April was heartily approved of by the New Jersey representatives in Congress. Despite their overwhelming Whig leanings, the various congressmen of the state approved of the opening of hostilities in a way that was an opposite reaction to the War of 1812. The voters of the state as well, though having gone against Polk in the 1844 election, seem to have generally supported the campaigns out west. A month after the formal declaration of war, the Whig governor of the state, Charles C. Stratton, issued a call for the organizing of militias. His calls were mirrored by President Polk, who requested five companies from the state in April 1847. That same month, when news arrived of the great victory of Taylor at Buena Vista, cannons were fired off in the Commons in Trenton to celebrate.

A recruiting station was established in Trenton in the Fort Rawnsley Hotel at the junction of Warren and Lamberton Streets. Set up on January 1, 1847, it very quickly drafted twenty-five to thirty men, who were paraded up and down the street, impressing the local citizens. On March 15, the station was relocated to Newark to continue the process of raising men in the northern part of the state. The various soldiers who were acquired were eventually mustered into the Tenth Infantry Regiment under Colonel Robert E. Temple, who had served as an aide-de-camp to Scott in Florida. The men made up E Company under Captain Samuel Dickinson, G Company drawn from Mercer County under Captain Yard, and H Company from Camden under Captain Joshua Collett. These units proceeded to Fort Hamilton on Staten Island for training, with G and H Companies afterward sailing on the *G.B. Lamar* for Matamoros, Mexico, which was reached on May 5. E Company eventually joined them a month later in June. An additional four companies were raised in September 1847 and organized as the New Jersey Battalion of Volunteers. With Lieutenant Colonel Dickinson Woodruff in charge, the New Jersey Battalion likewise traveled to Fort Hamilton for initial organization. Departing on September 24, 1847, aboard the *Senator*, the battalion arrived in Vera Cruz after a stormy voyage six weeks later. The trip was not without its incidents, however, including a riot among the men. The *Trenton News* reported: "We understand that a portion of the men of the New Jersey battalion, when required to go on board yesterday to sail for the seat of war, mutinied and stoned the officers. This was owing to the treatment that Captain Napton was received from the Colonel. When our informant left the riot had been quelled."[83]

Yet in the end, the New Jersey troops arrived after the cessation of most major combat operations. While the various companies of the Tenth and the New Jersey Battalion did suffer almost fifty casualties, these were all from accidents or disease. Perhaps most violent was the death of Captain Collett of H Company, who died in a duel with another army officer. By July 1848, the New Jersey Battalion arrived back at Fort Hamilton aboard the *Indianapolis*, while the various companies of the Tenth eventually staggered home.

The most notable death of the war was probably that of Captain Jacob Zabriskie, originally of Hackensack. After dying heroically at the Battle of Buena Vista as part of the regular army, his body was escorted back to New Jersey with the highest honors. His corpse was given parades in New Brunswick, where it was accompanied by the students and professors of Rutgers; New York City; and Bergen County. Gun salutes, honor guards, the mayor of New York City, a brass band from Paterson and a black funeral pall bearing the words "Buena Vista" in silver lettering all crowned the funeral parades. Reverend Cornelius T. Demarest eulogized thusly: "This brave son of New Jersey, in the hour of trial, has not dishonored his name and state. In the war of the revolution, waged for true liberty, just laws, a good government, a peaceful and happy home, New Jersey had a name. In this war with Mexico, for just causes and desirable ends, the name of 'Jersey Blue' remains untarnished." A large monument for the deceased still overlooks the Hackensack Courthouse today. The excessive

Philip Kearny lost his left arm in the Mexican War. *National Archives.*

fawning over a soldier of Manifest Destiny in a heavily Democratic county was used to help push politics that year. In fact, that same year, former governor Daniel Haines of Essex County won the gubernatorial election despite the Whig's retention of the assembly.

The state did produce various heroes in the army and navy during the conflict. Nathan Beakes Russell, Samuel Gibbs French, George Clinton Westcott, Harvey Brown and Lewis Golding Arnold all received congressional awards and accolades for their actions in the war. Also of note was Lieutenant Charles G. Hunter, who, while in command of the USS *Scourge*, managed to seize Alvarado and Flacotalpam without any bloodshed. His commander, Matthew Perry, had him court-martialed for acting beyond his orders, yet back in New Jersey, he received a silver pitcher depicting his victories at a Fourth of July parade in Trenton.

Perhaps the state's greatest contribution to the Mexican War were four of its finest sons. Stephen W. Kearny of Newark was a descendant of Lord Stirling and served in the War of 1812 before helping to organize the U.S. Cavalry out west. In August 1846, Colonel Kearny took Santa Fe, New Mexico, before marching onward to California. There he met up with Commodore Robert F. Stockton of Princeton, who had just recently seized California. Stockton had three years before overseen the construction of the first steam-powered warship in the navy, the USS *Princeton*. Kearny helped to organize that territory as well before succumbing to either malaria or yellow fever in 1848. Both men were surpassed in rank and accomplishment, though, by General Winfield Scott, whose pioneering amphibious invasion helped to move the army inland from Vera Cruz and secure Mexico City in September 1847. Finally, Philip Kearny, who had been schooled in France in cavalry tactics, proved himself to be one of the most flamboyant commanders of the campaign. Wounded at the Battle of Churubusco, he had his left arm amputated. Continuing to charge headfirst into combat with a saber in one hand and the reins between his teeth, he earned the respect of all around him. Scott once referred to him as "the bravest man I ever knew." The day Mexico City fell, he had the prestige of being the first American through the gate.

Manifest Destiny helped to define the future of the United States. The country would be a bi-coastal nation dominated for the next twenty years by the issue of the admission of slave and free states to its union. The sons of New Jersey played their part in this campaign as they had in previous ones, providing leadership, soldiers and the products of its mills and fields.

CHAPTER 6

TWICE AGAINST LINCOLN: THE CIVIL WAR IN NEW JERSEY

New Jersey has an interesting history concerning the Civil War. At the time, many considered the state pro-Southern rather than pro-Union. In fact, the *New York Times* summarized the situation thusly: "For, as Australia is in geography, so is New-Jersey in politics—an exception to all general laws. Its only correlative may in fact be found on the other side of Mason and Dixon's line. New-Jersey is the South Carolina of the North."[84] Yet at the same time, this alleged Copperhead state would send 10 percent of its population off to war. By the end of the conflict, thirty-four of its sons had received the Medal of Honor, and over six thousand had given the ultimate sacrifice in almost every major battle of the war. New Jersey's factories and mills produced the weapons and goods needed, while its citizens toiled in them and in the fields for victory.

In the antebellum period, New Jersey had a complicated relationship with slavery and the South. It was the last Northern state to end slavery; for though it had banned the practice in 1804, this ban was only gradual. In fact, by 1830, the majority of slaves in the North were still in New Jersey. Even after the absolute abolishment of the practice in 1846, "apprentices for life" continued to be found within the state. As late as the start of the war, eighteen were known to be residing in New Jersey. Yet at the same time, the state was a main thoroughfare along the Underground Railroad. Perhaps its most famous conductor, Harriet Tubman, came to Cape May in 1852, three years after her escape from Maryland. She went on to work at the Congress Hall Hotel as a cook, using much of the money she made to help finance the escape of other slaves from the South.

The state as a whole was closely connected to the society and economy of the South. Wealthy slave owners vacationed in Cape May, as did such presidents as Franklin Pierce and James Buchanan, both of whom lodged at the Congress Hall Hotel, undoubtedly eating food prepared by Tubman and other escaped slaves. Princeton University, the most southern of the Ivy League schools, possessed a Dixie-heavy enrollment every year. In addition, many of its first presidents had been slave owners, and much of its early finances was invested in slavery-related enterprises. While the cities of Paterson, Newark and Trenton were becoming models of modernization, this industrial economy became largely based on acquiring cheap materials from the South and then utilizing that same region as a marketplace for finished products. Disruption to slavery or a shattering of the Union, it was feared, could damage the economy of New Jersey.

Politically, though Republican Charles Smith Olden was elected governor of the state in 1859, he did so as a candidate of the "Opposition Party" in order to avoid being associated with more radical elements of the national Republican Party. Not surprisingly, in the 1860 presidential election, New Jersey became the only Northern state not to go fully for Lincoln, splitting its votes between him and Stephan Douglas. That same year, Representative William Pennington of Newark, who was currently Speaker of the House, lost his seat to Democrat Nehemiah Perry, a man well known for his business connections with the South.

During the war, politics in the state continued to remain staunchly Democratic. In 1862, Joel Parker was elected the new governor as a War Democrat, receiving 57 percent of the vote and carrying all but seven southern counties. Throughout the conflict, New Jersey remained the only Northern state with a Democratic governor and legislature, two Democratic senators and a majority of Democrats representing it in the House. In 1864, it became one of only two states to vote for General George McClellan against Lincoln. The former had been ordered to Trenton following his removal after the Antietam Campaign and became a lifelong, popular resident of the state, eventually serving as governor.

Anger at Lincoln and the Republicans sometimes ran deep in the state, with the *Monmouth Democrat* once asking why the president's son was "sporting away his college vacations at Long Branch" rather than

118

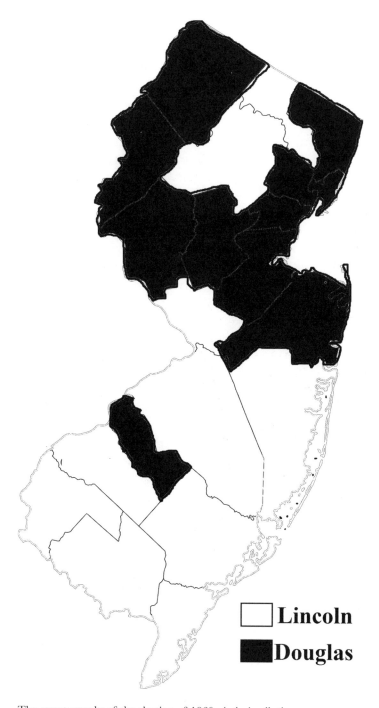

The county results of the election of 1860. *Author's collection.*

General George McClellan, New Jersey's choice for president in 1864. *National Archives.*

fighting in the war.[85] In 1861, the *Newark Daily Journal* pressed for immediate secession, while later on, it attacked the draft as a tyrannical overstep of power. Lincoln, during his inaugural train procession through Newark on his way to Washington, would have witnessed an effigy of himself hanging from a lamppost of the city.[86] Numerous residents were also arrested for anti-Union activities. Most notable among these was Mayor James Walter Wall of Burlington, who was arrested in September 1861 for treason and held at Fort Lafayette for several weeks. A few citizens even enlisted in the Confederate army, most notably George Washington Helme, who distinguished himself at Shiloh and went on to found the borough of Helmetta, New Jersey, after the war, and Julius De Lagnel of Newark, who rose to the rank of second in command of the Confederate Ordinance Bureau.

Yet despite all of its political or moral misgivings, many New Jersey residents and leaders responded loyally and enthusiastically to the call of the president for troops after the fall of Fort Sumter. By April, regular military gatherings and processions could be seen at Military Park in Newark. As early as May 4, 1861, the War Department requested three regiments from the state. New Jersey quickly raised the First, Second and Third Regiments at Camp Olden in Trenton, and soldiers from the state were the first to parade for President Lincoln in front of the White House that summer. Under the command of Brigadier General Theodore Runyon of Somerville as the Fourth Division of the Army of Northeastern Virginia, the three New Jersey regiments and an additional four regiments of militia were even present at the first major battle of the war, Bull Run. Other units raised that year, including the Tenth Regiment, which was better known as Olden's Legion, helped to build the fortifications around Washington meant to protect the nation's capital. These redoubts included the appropriately named Fort Kearny, which was constructed in 1862.

The only New Jersey units to see actual combat in 1861 were those assigned to Brigadier General Ambrose Burnside's Coastal Division, which had begun a campaign against coastal North Carolina. The Ninth New Jersey under Lieutenant Colonel Charles Heckman was the last of the units raised that year to leave the state but became the first to face enemy fire. On February 8, 1862, the unit made a rugged march through the swamps of Roanoke Island to outflank a Confederate position and achieve victory. Their mud-slogged advance earned them the nickname "Muskrats" from Burnside, a *nom de guerre* that they would maintain throughout the war. The unit continued to aid in the campaign, helping to take New Bern in March 1862 before being moved to South Carolina the following year. This operation was carried out as part of New Jersey resident General Winfield Scott's Anaconda Plan, the strategy that would eventually help win the war for the North.

McClellan's infamous Peninsula Campaign of 1862 also saw troops from New Jersey committed to battle. This time it was the Second New Jersey Brigade, originally under Colonel Samuel H. Starr, as part of Heintzelman's III Corps. They participated in most of the battles of the campaign, helping to besiege Yorktown, leading a direct assault on Fort Magruder and assaulting the Confederates at Seven Pines. They were also heavily involved in the Seven Days Battles. The Battle of Gaines' Mill, fought on June 27, 1862, saw the highest casualties yet for the First New Jersey Brigade. "It is rather hot in there," exclaimed Colonel Isaac Tucker as he led his men into the woods near the center of the battle. Only 965 of the 2,800 Jersey Blues who entered the woods emerged at the end of the battle. Most of the Fourth New Jersey was captured, and many fine officers, including Tucker, were killed. Despite its green status, the various regiments from the Garden State proved to be well disciplined and more than proved themselves in battle. Governor Olden, hearing of the exploits of his citizens, wrote to Colonel Starr in July that "the regiment was brave, and I have reason to congratulate myself in having command of as gallant a regiment as any in the service."[87] Perhaps the greatest showing by the state came in the form of Brigadier General Philip Kearny, whose wild charges and skilled leadership earned him the respect of both sides. "I'm a one-armed Jersey son-of-a-gun—follow me!" screamed Kearny as he charged into the fray at Williamsburg, and follow the men did.

Following the failure of McClellan's campaign, Lincoln pushed for another invasion of northern Virginia. Various units from New Jersey, including the Fifth–Eighth Regiments, were involved in the subsequent defeat at the Second Battle of Bull Run in August 1862. A few days prior, the First New Jersey Brigade under General George W. Taylor of High Bridge collided with Stonewall Jackson's corps. The various New Jersey units were defeated, and Taylor himself would eventually die from wounds he received at the battle. Yet a far greater loss for the state came a few days later at the Battle of Chantilly. During a violent storm, General Philip Kearny rode into a Confederate unit, where he was shot and killed. Mourned by friend and foe alike, Confederate general A.P.

Lieutenant Henry Van Ness of New Jersey, a member of the First U.S. Hussars. *U.S. Army Military History Institute.*

Hill remarked, "You've killed Phil Kearny...he deserved a better fate than to die in the mud." Lee had Kearny's body returned to Union lines, and he was eventually interred at Arlington National Cemetery. Kearny is represented by one of only two equestrian statues in that famous cemetery, and his figure also stands as one of the two states representing New Jersey in the U.S. Capitol's Statuary Hall.

The Battle of Fredericksburg, fought that winter, saw the commitment of eighteen regiments of infantry from New Jersey to battle, as did the subsequent "Mud March" that followed. The state continued to be represented in most major engagements of the war, including at Chancellorsville, where the Seventh New Jersey Volunteers captured five Confederate flags, and in the Gettysburg Campaign. In the latter, units from the state fought at such famous segments of the battlefield as Devil's Den, the Wheatfield and the Peach Orchard. Monuments have been erected on the battlefield to the Sixth Regiment at Devil's Den and to the Twelfth "Buck and Ball" as well. At the start of the battle, Garden State resident Horatio Stockton Howell, a chaplain and medical aid, was notoriously shot dead by a Confederate skirmisher. John Burns, born in Burlington in 1794, became the oldest soldier on the field and, despite being turned down for active service, grabbed his musket and marched out to meet the enemy. Wounded and briefly captured by the Confederates, he became a national hero and accompanied Lincoln during his visit to the field in 1863. During the emergency that attended this campaign, Governor Parker called up two battalions of volunteer militia who were dispatched to Pennsylvania to help stem the Confederate advance while other temporary units were organized in the state under Richard Stockton. New Jersey continued to send men to the eastern theater in Virginia for the next two years, including a number of one-hundred-day regiments that were called up by Lincoln to help prosecute the siege of Petersburg in the last year of the war.

The enlistment of black soldiers proved to be a controversial issue in many states, but possibly nowhere more so than in New Jersey. Congressman Nehemiah Perry challenged Lincoln and Radical Republicans after the passage of the Emancipation Proclamation, criticizing them for not loving the country "better than the negro."[88] Following this, the state's legislature passed a measure disproving of the act, the only one in the North to do so, and attempted to pass a bill to expel all blacks who moved to the state. New Jersey took a further step in March 1864 when the state senate introduced a bill to fine those

Congressman Nehemiah Perry, who replaced Speaker William Pennington after the latter's loss in 1860. *Library of Congress.*

Spencer Union Church in Woodstown, New Jersey, where many black Civil War veterans are buried. *Library of Congress.*

who attempted to enlist black soldiers. Though no black regiments were raised by the state, 2,900 of its citizens did travel to other states to join the army. One of these, George Ashby of Crosswicks, would even go on to be the oldest surviving veteran in the state, dying at the age of 102 in 1946.

Other notable residents of the state include Captain Michael Gallagher of the Second New Jersey Cavalry, who took part in the massively successful escape from Libby Prison in Richmond in February 1864. The prison had an additional connection to this state when, in 1863, the Confederate government, in response to the shooting of two of its captured officers, announced that it would execute two Northern soldiers. One of these men drawn by lottery was Henry Sawyer of New Jersey, the eventual owner of the Chalfonte Hotel in Cape May, who had been captured at the Battle of Brandy Station. Sawyer's wife traveled across the country to personally lobby President Lincoln for his release. Thanks to appeals by the president and a variety of threats by Secretary of War Stanton, the standoff was eventually resolved.

The state also boasted its own Florence Nightingale in the form of Cornelia Hancock, who helped to nurse soldiers at Gettysburg. In the field of the arts, one of the more important names is Ellen Clementine Howarth of Trenton, who penned "My Jersey Blue" in 1864.

My Jersey Blue

Yes, here my heroes come on crutches,
With bandaged head and empty sleeves;
And though this sight my warm heart touches,
'Tis not for him alone I grieve.
O not for him who scorned to falter,
Though in the thickest of the strife!
Nor yet for him who on the altar
Of our loved country laid his life.
Are we not children of one mother?
Are we not to the Union true?
You fought for it, my soldier brother!
I pray for it, my Jersey Blue!

Lilly Martin Spencer of Newark used her skills as an artist to help produce patriotic paintings for the war effort, while Thomas Nast of Morristown drew hundreds of political cartoons and was proclaimed by Lincoln to be his "best recruiting sergeant." In Perth Amboy, Rebecca Buffum Spring, a noted abolitionist, turned her home into a military academy to help train officers for the war. In the field of foreign affairs, New Jersey supplied two of the most important diplomats of the war: Senator William L. Dayton from Basking Ridge, who served as minister to France and helped to keep Napoleon III out of the war, and Thomas H. Dudley, who worked to prevent Confederate commerce raiders from departing from Liverpool.

Perhaps the most notorious resident of the state to serve in the war was Hugh Judson Kilpatrick of Wantage. Called "Kill-cavalry" by many contemporaries, the Jersey native was a skilled horseman known for his often-suicidal rides into enemy formations. Kilpatrick helped to ravage Lee's supply lines during the Chancellorsville Campaign, while at Gettysburg he led a criticized charge against Longstreet's flank west of Little Round Top. His most infamous moment came with the Dahlgren Affair in 1864. Kilpatrick orchestrated a badly planned raid deep into

Confederate territory to free Union prisoners around Richmond. The failed attack gained notoriety for the papers found on the body of Colonel Ulric Dahlgren, which seemed to order the execution of Jefferson Davis and his entire cabinet. Though pronounced by many as a forgery, the letters doomed Kilpatrick's career in the East and possibly set in motion Lincoln's own assassination a year later. William Tecumseh Sherman did take notice of the bold New Jersey cavalryman, stating, "I know that Kilpatrick is a hell of a damned fool, but I want just that sort of man to command my cavalry on this expedition." Years after the war, in order to drum up support for his political ambitions, Kilpatrick even organized the first Civil War reenactment in August 1878. Over forty thousand people are said to have attended the mock battle in Wantage, New Jersey, at which over ten thousand barrels of beer were served.

Despite some initial economic shocks from the secession of the South, New Jersey industry responded as patriotically as its citizens to the advent of war. Major cities such as Paterson and Camden thrived economically, thanks to contracts for guns and uniforms. John Boylan of Newark received over $5 million worth of contracts for uniforms, while Henry Sauerbier, whose Newark-based factory had produced cutlery before the war, turned its attention to swords and bayonets.[89] Nathan Barnert of Paterson also produced countless uniforms for the Union, while Rogers, Ketchner & Grosvenor Locomotive manufactured the trains that helped to transport the Northern armies and their supplies. At the height of the war, the Rogers Works on Spruce Street in Paterson could produce between ten and twelve completed engines a month. Trenton boasted the cutlery company of James Emerson, which turned out swords for the war, while Charles Hewitt's ironworks manufactured one thousand rifle barrels a week for Trenton-Springfield Rifle.

The state's naval heritage is again evident during the Civil War, as its shipyards roared into action. Zeno Secor, who already had a shipyard in Manhattan, opened up a dockyard in Jersey City. Along with Joseph Colwell, to whom Secor outsourced some of his contracts, Secor helped to build a number of monitor warships. Among these were the *Passaic*-class ships *Montauk*, *Weehawken* and *Camanche*, which were launched starting in 1862. The following year, Secor constructed the *Canonicus*-class vessels *Tecumseh*, *Mahopac* and *Manhattan*. In a feat of engineering success, the New Jersey company built the *Camanche* to be disassembled. It was then shipped to California by sea and reassembled in the Pacific, allowing the United States to become the first nation with an ironclad in

Cavalryman Hugh Judson Kilpatrick of Sussex County. Library of Congress.

that ocean. Additional ships were constructed at Camden, Keyport and various other locations throughout the state.

In addition to ships, New Jersey also contributed many naval commanders of note to the war. Included among these were Commander Charles S. Boggs, who received widespread acclaim for his actions aboard

A Civil War locomotive of the style made in Paterson, New Jersey. *Library of Congress.*

the USS *Varuna* during the Battle of New Orleans. After destroying six Confederate vessels, Boggs beached his heavily damaged ship and continued to fire upon enemy forces in the area until the *Varuna* finally submerged. At the same battle, Commodore James Shedden Palmer of Elizabethtown commanded the USS *Iroquois* and helped to clear

Deck of the USS *Passaic*, built in New Jersey. *Library of Congress.*

New Orleans and push up toward Vicksburg. Captain Tunis Augustus MacDonald Craven, who conducted the surveys of the Isthmus of Darien that would allow for the subsequent construction of the Panama Canal, heroically died when his ship, the USS *Tecumseh*, was sunk at Mobile Bay in 1864.[90]

Despite the Union's complete dominance of the seas, there was still fear throughout New Jersey of actions by the Confederate navy. The construction of the CSS *Virginia* in 1862 allowed the South to plan an audacious breakout and subsequent attack on New York City. Only the timely arrival of the *Monitor* and subsequent battle at Hampton Roads prevented the potential shelling of Manhattan. The arrival of the CSS *Alabama* that fall off the eastern seaboard further spread fear throughout New Jersey. Captain Semmes prowled the coast of New York and New Jersey for weeks, taking prizes and threatening to assault New York City itself. These incidents proved to be a catalyst for increased shipbuilding and the shoring up of harbor defenses throughout the region. The Stevens family of Hoboken again began construction on the *Stevens Battery*, a massive ironclad that had been under construction since the war scare of 1841. Twenty years before the construction of John Ericsson's *Monitor*, the Stevens family of New Jersey had received funding from the U.S. government under President John Tyler to construct their own ironclad warship, though in the end it was never completed. The USS *Passaic*, built in Brooklyn, even managed to attain a small level of notoriety in the state when, in November 1862, at the height of the *Alabama* scare, it was sailed up the Hudson to begin target practice on the Palisades. As New Jersey locals had not been forewarned about this, panic quickly broke out, and order was not restored for hours. The Palisades continued to be used by the navy during the course of the war as an ideal gunnery range for its new ironclads constructed in Jersey City and Manhattan.

The war officially ended for the state on May 2, 1866. On that day, the last New Jersey regiment to return to the state, the Thirty-fourth, arrived home in Trenton, having been posted to Alabama to help oversee issues of Reconstruction. So ended a conflict that saw over 88,000 of the state's men engaged in combat for almost five years. Over 6,200 of these men would never return home again. A rather famous nurse during the war and resident of New Jersey named Walt Whitman described his fellow citizens of the state as being "of real grit...I think the bulk of Jerseymen have as much as any people anywhere."[91]

CHAPTER 7

NEW JERSEY AND THE USS *MAINE*: THE GARDEN STATE IN THE AGE OF IMPERIALISM

The end of the Civil War saw a return to Manifest Destiny and an upsurge in the immigration and industrialization that had made the North so successful in the conflict. The state of New Jersey would again see every aspect of the American experience with the events of the era. In addition, as the nation began the slow buildup of its military in response to its increased presence in the world, so, too, did the Garden State.

In 1869, the New Jersey legislature passed a series of bills creating a state guard. This streamlined the various county militias, placing them more effectively under the control of the governor. The reorganization of the state military continued apace over the next two decades. In 1872, the state formed the Eighth Colored Infantry, which would serve until 1878. The seacoast of New Jersey was further secured thanks to the creation of the Sea Coast Artillery in 1877 and the New Jersey Naval Reserve in 1890. Governor George McClellan of Civil War fame continued the process of modernizing the troops of the state. In 1879, he approved, along with the governors of various other states, the creation of an effective National Guard model for New Jersey. McClellan then set about modernizing the force by equipping it with, among other things, two companies of Gatling guns.

Governor Thomas Fitz Randolph utilized this new body to help put down riots in both Camden County and Jersey City in 1871. During the Great Railroad Strike that rocked the nation in 1877, the guard was again called on to put down riots by construction gangs in Bergen County and to reopen the Pennsylvania Railroad in Phillipsburg. Additional units were called on to help safeguard other rail lines in the state and prevent their seizure by striking workers. Later that year, when violence erupted between Catholic and Protestants in Jersey City, the state's military was again used as a way to ensure peace.

The closing of the century witnessed the nation finishing its campaign of Manifest Destiny. Wars against the various Indian tribes of the West were drawn to a close, settlers seized on the last parcels of land and the great railroads of the nation tied the far corners of America together. Residents of New Jersey were again active in most battles and activities of the time period. Ten of its citizens would receive the Medal of Honor for actions out west, including Captain Edward Godfrey of Cookstown. Godfrey had served with the Seventh Cavalry at the Battle of Little Big Horn before receiving the nation's highest award for his actions against the Nez Perce. Yet perhaps his most notable achievement was his creation of the army's first Cooking and Baking School.

America's brief foray into imperialism saw the state of New Jersey again active in the defense of the nation. On February 15, 1898, the explosion of the USS *Maine* in Havana's harbor pushed both the nation and New Jersey slowly toward war. Of the 261 casualties that resulted from the ship's sinking, at least 15 were residents of New Jersey, with 5 other residents of the state being pulled from the water.[92] A memorial was eventually constructed in Pompton Lakes, complete with the ship's engine room funnel. Enthusiastic calls for action emerged from all parts of the nation. The German American Veteran's Association of South River and Sayreville wrote to President McKinley on February 27, 1898, that they were "ready to fight when you send for us. Ready at any time."[93] Yet despite the desire by most citizens of the nation to go to war, President McKinley was still reluctant to do so. It was to be largely the efforts of his vice president that pushed him toward that fateful decision. Garret Hobart of Paterson was a staunch internationalist and pleaded with McKinley to accept war with Spain before the Congress acted without him. Following the war, Hobart also famously cast the tiebreaking vote that claimed the Philippines for America rather than granting it independence, a decision that was to have immense consequence for America in 1941.

Once war was declared, the state responded dutifully to the requests of the government. As the *Elizabeth Daily Journal* opined of Governor Foster McGowan Voorhees, the war "offered a fine opportunity for him to display his abilities, and his work was so excellent that it overshadowed

Wreckage of the USS *Maine*, aboard which many New Jersey residents died. *Library of Congress.*

his subsequent activities."[94] With 4,297 men already under arms in the militia, and another 385,273 eligible to be called up, the state had the seventh-largest army in the nation.[95] Two days after a request by McKinley for 75,000 men, Voorhees called for the raising of four regiments of volunteers in the state and had the state legislature allocate $47,000 for their preparation. These men were raised and organized as the First Regiment of Newark, the Second Regiment of Paterson and Montclair, the Third Regiment of Elizabeth (augmented by companies from Rahway, New Brunswick, Asbury Park and Freehold) and the Fourth Regiment of Jersey City. Governor Voorhees ordered the men to be assembled at the aptly named Camp Voorhees in Sea Girt from May to July 1898 under General Joseph Plume, with the governor himself staying at the camp to help organize and prepare the soldiers. Patriotism was not limited to the troops or their elected leader, with a delegation of Civil War veterans from Merchantville presenting a regimental flag from the previous war to Secretary of War Alger to be raised over Morro Castle in Cuba. Though eager to fight, the men spent most of their time battling boredom and the torrential rain that visited the Jersey shore that

May. Regimental surgeons issued quinine as a precaution against the spread of malaria among the regiments. In May, President McKinley offered Senator William Sewell of Camden an appointment as a major general of the volunteers. Sewell had received a Medal of Honor for his actions at the Battle of Chancellorsville and commanded New Jersey troops at Gettysburg. Though he visited the camp at Sea Girt and talked strategy with Plume and Voorhees, Sewell eventually turned down the offer, as it would have entailed his relinquishing of his Senate seat. It seemed as if the men in the state's naval militia were to be the only ones from the state to fire their guns in earnest, as the patrol tug *Fred B. Dalzell* opened fire on the tug *Edward G. Burgess* on May 11 when the latter brazenly sailed into the minefield of the Narrows, disregarding orders from the War Department.

Eventually, after much waiting and wondering, the different units were ordered to various parts of the South from Virginia to Florida. Governor Voorhees, continuing his efforts in preparing the troops as much as possible, requested at least ten hours' notice from the Department of War in order to provide rations to the men for traveling. This move was aimed at correcting reported issues of a lack of supplies and victuals for units from New York and Massachusetts as they waited hours for transports in New York Harbor.

None of the infantry regiments would ever see combat in Cuba. The closest that the men of New Jersey came to conflict occurred stateside at Camp Alger in Dunn Loring, Virginia. As disease proved to be the deadliest factor at the camp, men of the Eighth Pennsylvania dug a well to provide fresh water for their regiment. On June 6, a fight broke out as men from the First New Jersey took the well at bayonet point. Lieutenant Charles Beecher of Pennsylvania then distributed ammunition to his men and retook the well by force. Officers of both regiments soon arrived and diffused the situation peacefully, thus ending the only combat seen by either unit during the war.

President McKinley arrived in late May to personally review the troops. During this visit, he inspected the First New Jersey, complimenting the men on their readiness and proud history. By August, the regiment was transferred to the Fourth Brigade of III Corps in preparation for the invasion of Puerto Rico. However, as the war soon ended, the men were instead mustered out of service on November 8, 1898. Overall, nine men were lost during the war at Camp Alger, all from disease and none from Spanish rifle fire.

Spanish-American War soldiers from New York and New Jersey. *Library of Congress.*

In fact, perhaps the largest loss of life from New Jersey during the war occurred not in Cuba or the Philippines but in Pompton Lakes. On July 12, 1898, an explosion tore through the Laflin-Rand Powder Works in Pompton Lakes, killing ten instantly and wounding two dozen others. Included among the dead was a soldier from the Third New Jersey Volunteers who had been posted with others to guard the vital factory from sabotage. The damage was estimated at $100,000 and took the plant out of operation for almost two weeks. The disaster was not the only one of the war for New Jersey. In April of that same year, the Atlantic Dynamite Company of Dover, which was mass-producing gunpowder for the various army units gathering in southern camps, suffered a massive explosion that killed six instantly. A second explosion took place two weeks later on May 10 at the same location. Fear of sabotage prompted both federal and state officials to call for increased security at such locations.

Hundreds of volunteers from the state also saw service at sea during the conflict. In May 1898, men of the state's Battalion of the West were sent to the Caribbean to serve aboard the USS *Resolute*. From this vantage point, they participated in the Battle of Santiago de Cuba, which saw the destruction of the Spanish fleet. On August 12, the ship was sent to bombard Manzanillo but received word the next day that an armistice had been signed. Additional men from the Battalion of the East were sent to the same theater to serve aboard the USS *Badger*, which would go on to take three prizes in Nuevitas Harbor. Three residents of the state even received Medals of Honor for their service aboard the USS *Marblehead* and *Nashville* during the extraordinary cutting of the cable at Cienfuegos, Cuba, on May 11, 1898. Ironically, and perhaps more importantly, many of the ships that these men would serve on were the direct result of the naval buildup by Secretary of the Navy George Maxwell Robeson of New Jersey, a man responsible for the modernization of the navy after the Virginius Affair in 1873.

Fear of an attack by the Spanish Home Fleet while the U.S. Navy was largely engaged in the Caribbean and Pacific prompted Washington to call into service various mothballed ships from the Civil War to protect the ports of the East Coast. The monitors *Mahopac* and *Manhattan* were sent to Philadelphia to protect the Delaware River, while the *Nahant* was sent to New York City and the *Sangamon* sailed to guard Fishers Island off Long Island. The USS *Ajax*, which had been docked at Camden while on loan to the New Jersey Naval Militia, was fired up on April 2 under the orders of Governor Voorhees. Three months later, the ship was recommissioned by the U.S. Navy and sent to help protect Baltimore. The *Hercules*, which had been launched in 1882 in Camden, was acquired by the navy, renamed the *Chickasaw* and sent to patrol the waters off South Carolina. Additional men from the state's Battalion of the West were sent to man the USS *Montauk*, then patrolling off Portland, and the USS *Venezuela* (*Panther*).

In addition, various antiquated fortifications around the state were updated to meet the demands of the war. Construction was again started on Fort Mott near Pennsville, which, though twenty years out of date, would have served as the front lines in the defense of the Delaware River. As part of the Endicott Era of defenses, Fort Hancock on Sandy Hook was upgraded to have disappearing guns powered by a steam hydraulic lift system that was capable of dealing significant damage to Spanish ships. In late May, General Royal T. Frank called up over four hundred

The USS *Panther* helped to seize Guantanamo Bay and carried a crew from New Jersey. *Library of Congress.*

men from the Third New Jersey Regiment to man the fortifications at Sandy Hook. Finally, batteries at various towns along the shore, including at Sea Girt, were readied for any possible action.

The state also became the prime location for war propaganda, thanks to perhaps its most famous resident at the time. Thomas Edison, inventor of the motion picture, used his equipment to film a variety of anti-Spanish propaganda films in New Jersey in the lead-up to the war. Depicting the atrocities committed by the enemy in Cuba, these movies helped to further turn public support toward war. During the actual fighting, Edison set about creating six reenactment films in New Jersey depicting the Battle of Manila and the subsequent fighting against Filipino insurgents. Though shot in the Garden State and employing African Americans as Filipinos, the movies were still widely popular with the general population and helped to show the power of film in war. A few months after the end of the war, Guglielmo Marconi built the first wireless antenna atop the Twin Lights at Navesink. Using his invention, he was able to broadcast to residents of the state the return of the victorious Commodore George Dewey, hero of Manila.

Perhaps the most important contribution of the state to the various wars of imperialism waged by the nation continued to be its shipbuilding industry. The Crescent Shipyard of Elizabeth was opened in 1895 by Lewis Nixon and Arthur Leopold Busch. Over the course of the next

Inventor John P. Holland aboard his submarine, the USS *Holland*. *U.S. Naval Institute.*

two decades, Nixon would design and turn out such ships as the gunboats *Nicholson* and *O'Brien*; the cruiser *Chattanooga*, which had the honor of returning John Paul Jones's remains from France in 1905; the monitor *Florida*; and the gunboat *Annapolis*, which fought at the Battle of Nipe Bay and was later used to support troops during the Philippine Insurrection. Most notable among its creations were the first submarines to enter service in the U.S. Navy. In 1894, Simon Lake of Pleasantville designed and launched the *Argonaut Jr.*, which was followed four years later by the *Argonaut*. During the fall of 1898, at the height of the Spanish-American War, Lake sailed his submarine from Norfolk to Sandy Hook. In 1897, Crescent Shipyard and John P. Holland of Paterson constructed the submarine USS *Holland*. The ship was eventually purchased by the navy in 1900 and used to construct the subsequent *Plunger*, or *A-Class* of submarines. Five of the seven ships of this line would be built in Elizabeth and would be sent to the Philippines to serve American interests in the Pacific during World War I. Lewis Nixon also established the International Smokeless Powder and Dynamite Company in Sayreville, which produced munitions for the war before being acquired by DuPont in 1904.

Other industries also flourished during the brief war. One such business was the Norfolk and New Brunswick Hosiery Company, which received a contract to provide 9,600 woolen shirts to the navy. Factories in Paterson, Camden and Newark roared into action as well, producing tents, uniforms and other military essentials.

In an interesting side note, eighteen years after the war, at the height of the Jersey shark attacks of 1916, one captain put forward an interesting though implausible explanation for the incidents. He claimed that a Spanish shark from the Caribbean had been driven up north by the bombing during the Spanish-American War. Many papers at the time carried this story of almost divine retribution for the conquest of Cuba.[96]

CHAPTER 8

SABOTAGE AND SUBMARINES:
NEW JERSEY AND THE GREAT WAR

The advent of the world wars, rather than removing the danger of conflict to foreign fields, placed New Jersey on the front lines of danger in a way it had not been since the American Revolution. While no battles would take place on its soil, the Garden State's unique geographic position, industrial nature and ethnic makeup made it a prime target for German sabotage and irregular warfare.

Like most other states at the time, New Jersey had a large population that could claim German descent. Even to this day, German heritage remains the predominant ethnic background of Americans. German newspapers flourished in the state, including the *New Jersey Free Newspaper*, which was considered to be the most influential German-language paper in the country at the time. Newark was home to a number of breweries and produced more lager per capita than any other city in the nation. Finally, the state's very location, fronting Ellis Island, ensured a steady stream of German immigrants. Thus, it comes as no surprise that as World War I heated up and the United States drifted closer toward involvement in the conflict, New Jersey became a prime target for the Kaiser.

Dozens of factories and shipyards existed in the state or sprang up during the Great War to satisfy the demands of the Allies. New York Shipbuilding in Camden, for example, would eventually grow to become the largest corporation of its type in the nation. Some of the many vessels that it turned out included the battleships *Michigan, Utah, Arkansas* and *Oklahoma*, as well as numerous destroyers. The company grew so large during the war that a federally funded, planned community called Yorkship Village was constructed in Camden. A total of one thousand model homes were built for workers and their families to accommodate the expanding workforce of the shipyard. The state also hosted numerous gunpowder and shell factories, many dangerously close to civilian areas.

Count Johann von Bernstorff, the German ambassador to the United States who was also covertly in charge of that nation's sabotage efforts against America, began to recruit terrorists and pick out industrial targets across the nation. Over the course of the war, it is estimated that over two hundred individual acts of terrorism were committed against the United States, with twenty-eight taking place in New York and New Jersey. Once again, due to the industrial nature of the state, one of the first acts occurred in January 1915 in Trenton with the fire at the Roebling Wire and Cable Plant.

For over three hours, a raging fire leveled not only eight acres of factory but also fourteen homes belonging to the workers. The outmatched Trenton Fire Department had to seek help from other local companies, including some from Camden, almost thirty miles away. It was truly a miracle that none of the workers were killed. An investigation after the fire revealed that the wires to the fire alarm had been cut. Ten months later, the scenario played itself out again as another fire reduced the company's machine shop on Hamilton Avenue to ashes and rubble. Again the fire alarm had been cut, and again the workers escaped without injury. Though arson by German agents was suspected at the time, no major investigation was ever undertaken. Yet as Roebling was the major supplier of antisubmarine netting and other materials to the Allies, suspecting the Germans of involvement would not be incredulous. One of the lead German agents in the country, Franz von Rintelen, wrote that American industry was "a spectre, an intangible phantom, against which strategy, tactics and all the courage of the German soldier were helpless." Against such an enemy, sabotage was perhaps the only answer.[97]

In July 1916, the state was terrorized for twelve days by a series of fatal shark attacks that claimed the lives of four people. The fear of German sabotage and attack was so palpable at the time that some even went so far as to blame the Kaiser for the brutal maulings along the shore. The *New York Times* reported, "These sharks may have devoured human bodies in the waters of the German war zone and followed liners to this coast, or even followed the *Deutschland* herself, expecting the usual toll of drowning men, women, and children…this would account for their boldness and their craving for human flesh."[98] Obviously, the idea of sharks trailing submarines was ludicrous, but the image seized upon the public so much that newspapers of the day began depicting both U-boats and politicians as sharks in their editorial cartoons.

A worse attack was to come only a few weeks later at the end of July in 1916. Just after midnight, a detective patrolling the docks of Black Tom Island noticed several fires on the pier and alerted the Jersey City Fire Department. Largely a misnomer, the island was actually a landfill pier that extended into New York Harbor. For the past few years, it had become a depot for war materials being shipped to the Allies and, as such, was undoubtedly a tempting target for the Germans. Somewhere between 2 to 4 million pounds of explosives were sitting in railroad cars on the pier, while the ship *Johnson Barge No. 19*, which was illegally tied up at the docks, held 100,000 pounds of explosives in its hold and 417 cases of fuses. Despite this treasure-trove of munitions, there were only a handful of guards on duty patrolling the area.

Though the JCPD tried its best to fight the blaze, the fire quickly grew out of hand and soon reached the explosives stored around the island. At 2:08 a.m., a massive explosion ripped through the island. Metal from the warehouses and shells mixed with wood from the dock formed a lethal barrage of shrapnel that blanketed Hudson County and Manhattan. Windows were shattered in New York City, the *Jersey Journal* building's clock was permanently stopped at 2:12 a.m., the beautiful stained-glass windows of St. Patrick's in Jersey City were destroyed, the ceilings of the Hudson County Courthouse and Assembly were ruined and even the Statue of Liberty was damaged. The blast was so strong that the Brooklyn Bridge swayed from side to side and the windshields of cars crossing the span exploded.

Fear quickly spread through the area, as an attack by an enemy nation was feared. Phone lines soon went dead in both Manhattan and Jersey City, only adding to the chaos. At least four people were killed after the explosion, including a ten-week-old child in Jersey City who was thrown from his crib by the shockwave. The total damage was estimated to be about $20 million (roughly $400 million in today's money), with thirteen warehouses, six piers and hundreds of rail cars destroyed. The Germans obviously denied all involvement, going so far as to blame the guard's lighting of small fires to drive away mosquitoes for the conflagration, and it would not be until 1953 that the nation finally agreed to pay $50

Wreckage of Black Tom Island in Jersey City following the terrorist attack. *AP photo.*

Camp Evans Radio Transmitter, 1921. Among those pictured is Albert Einstein. *Franklin Township Public Library Archives.*

million in reparations. Despite the massive scope of the attack and its effect on the largest city in America, the nation continued to remain neutral in the conflict raging across the ocean.

Six months later, another German attack took place on New Jersey's soil. On January 11, 1917, a fire broke out at Kingsland, a huge forty-acre factory complex in the Meadowlands of Lyndhurst. Owned by the Canadian Car and Foundry Company, the plant produced an astonishing 3 million shells per month, most headed for the Eastern Front. Perhaps due to lessons learned from Roebling and Black Tom Island, the plant was surrounded by a six-foot fence, which was constantly patrolled by guards. Workers were searched every day on entering the factory to make sure they were not carrying matches or anything else that could be used to ignite the shells stored there. A German agent managed to get hired at Kingsland and was assigned to Building 30, which handled the cleaning of the completed shell casings. With the ample amount of alcohol and oil used in the process, this man was ideally situated to destroy the entire complex.

On a chilly day in January, a fire broke out in Building 30 that quickly spread throughout the complex. The estimated 500,000 completed artillery shells in the area quickly began to explode, spreading the fire and increasing the damage. The heroine of the day was Tessie McNamara, the first female employee of the company. Working the switchboard, she stayed at her post while shells rocketed around her in order to warn every building of the fire. Newspapers at the time stated that all 1,700 employees escaped alive, with many fleeing across the frozen Hackensack River.

After four hours, the entire forty-acre complex was destroyed. The fire spread up the hill and destroyed residential homes in the town of Lyndhurst as well. Across the river at Snake Hill, residents of the insane asylum began to panic until Dr. George King and Dr. James Meehan rushed in with ice cream and candy, telling the patients that the Great War had ended and what they were seeing was a victory celebration. All in all, while the efforts of McNamara and others averted large-scale casualties, the shells meant for Russia would never arrive. Even worse, the entire Kingsland facility was effectively out of the war, and the company lost an estimated $12 million in damages. Germany had again attacked New Jersey.

The final major incident of terrorism to hit the Garden State during World War I occurred toward the end of the conflict. On October 4, 1918,

Franklin W. Martin of East Orange (left), who was awarded the Croix de Guerre. *Private collection.*

at around 7:30 p.m., an explosion rocked the T.A. Gillespie Shell Loading Plant in Morgan, New Jersey. Considered by many to be the largest such facility on the planet, the gradual destruction of the various factories and warehouses took three days to accomplish. The two thousand workers on the night shift quickly fled in terror following the initial blast but were soon followed by most of the residents of Sayreville and South Amboy. As the ground continued to shake, large sections of Perth Amboy were evacuated as well. Various Coast Guard units stationed in Raritan Bay helped to evacuate citizens, with twelve sailors being awarded the Navy Cross and two dying during the operation.

Casualties have been notoriously hard to estimate from the disaster, but most sources argue that over one hundred were killed and hundreds more injured. One mass grave in Old Bridge alone holds the remains of fourteen to eighteen unidentified persons. The outbreak of Spanish influenza the following year hit the region perhaps harder than most other parts of the state due to the continued presence of so many homeless crowded together in shelters. The streaming of refugees heading in all directions from Morgan was the closest America came to experiencing similar scenes of mass evacuations across the ocean in Europe during the war.

The German war against America was not confined to the factories of New Jersey. Once the nation entered the conflict, the coastal waterways of the state again became a target for raiding in a way that they had not been since the Civil War. The German submarine *U-151*, the first to enter American waters, scored its most spectacular successes off the coast of New Jersey in 1918. Over the course of its campaign along the eastern seaboard, *U-151* sunk twenty-three ships. Its greatest day came on June 2, 1918, in what became known as Black Sunday. In only a few hours, the German crew sunk six ships and laid a barrage of mines that would cripple the tanker *Herbert L. Pratt* the following day. Over fourteen thousand tons of cargo and ship was sent to the bottom of the Atlantic with thirteen seamen dying after a lifeboat from the SS *Caroline* capsized.[99] These deaths off the coast of Atlantic City were the first in American waters from submarine activity during the war. In a similar vein, the SS *Gulflight*, which had been built in Camden, became the first American ship to suffer casualties from a German submarine attack. Sailing out of Port Arthur loaded with gasoline for France in 1915, the boat was stopped by British warships on suspicion of working with the Germans and was being escorted back to English waters when a U-boat surfaced

Gas mask training at Fort Dix, New Jersey. *Library of Congress.*

and fired on the tanker. Three Americans were killed in the incident, becoming the first loss of life for the nation in the war at sea.

Perhaps due to the various acts of suspected German terrorism that plagued the state, local and federal authorities began to target citizens of New Jersey as potential traitors. The Espionage Act of 1917 and Sedition Act of 1918 had been crafted by Congress to help battle disloyal German Americans and others during the war. Benedict and Edwin Prieth, who published perhaps the most influential German-language newspaper in the nation, early on became targets for President Wilson. Both men were arrested and charged under the Espionage Act with hurting recruitment efforts. Despite their arrest and the shuttering of their paper, Benedict still received over two thousand votes in the election for Newark City commissioner that fall. In September 1918, both men finally made it to trial, only to be released due to a hung jury.

Yet the federal government was not so easily deterred. In September 1918, the U.S. Senate's Overman Committee began an investigation into the United States Brewers Association. During the hearings, Attorney

General A. Mitchell Palmer, who famously fought against encroachments by bolshevism and anarchism during the Red Scare of 1919, stressed the links between various brewers in the country and attempts to buy controlling shares in American newspapers in order to push German propaganda. By the end of his testimony, he would accuse twelve of the fifteen major German breweries in the nation, including those in Newark, of treasonous activities. The shock of the allegations were used to turn the Overman Committee into a more permanent body that would meet for months investigating various citizens and organizations for disloyalty.

But the government wasn't the only entity aimed at eradicating pro-German elements within society. The area of German Valley in Morris County officially changed its name to Long Valley during the war as part of a larger national trend aimed at rebranding German foods and companies. The residents of the state likewise made every effort in their politics to prepare for the coming conflict. In the 1916 presidential election, New Jersey went against native President Wilson, who campaigned on the platform of "He kept us out of war," in favor of Charles Evans Hughes, who ran on a promise of "Preparedness." Hughes won by a comfortable 10 percent margin, showing at least some desire among the citizens of New Jersey to prepare themselves to enter World War I. That same year, Republican Walter Evans Edge won the governorship over H. Otto Wittpenn. Undoubtedly, the very German-sounding named of his opponent also helped to contribute to Edge's victory.

As the nation came closer to war, so, too, did the state of New Jersey. Two weeks before Congress officially declared war, the state's assembly granted extraordinary military powers to Governor Edge. A state militia was quickly organized to replace the National Guard should the latter be federalized and sent overseas. To better help coordinate with various regional and local officials, Edge set up a Committee of Public Safety, which, as one of its first actions, recommended an increased security presence around key facilities in the state. In addition, concerns over the possible drafting of farm labor in the state led to the creation of a system by which high school youths were recruited to work harvesting local fields.

Perhaps the most important function of Edge's war government was to begin the process of acquiring land within the state for military bases. In June 1917, ground was broken for what eventually became Camp Dix. Named for Major General John Adams Dix, who had famously ordered U.S. Treasury agents in New Orleans to shoot anyone who attempted to pull down the American flag, the base was quickly taken over by the federal government to accommodate the Thirty-fourth, Seventy-eighth and Eighty-seventh Divisions. In August, local labor began work on the 770-acre Camp Merritt in Bergen County as well. Thanks to these two large bases, New Jersey quickly became the main embarkation point for soldiers sailing to the war in Europe. Over 3 million men would pass through Hoboken, giving rise to the popular saying that the men sailing to the war were promised either "heaven, hell, or Hoboken" as their return destination. The sheer number of out-of-state soldiers who inhabited the camps or gathered along the docks of Hoboken gave rise to the idea that New Jersey was "occupied territory." Concerns over the actions of these unsupervised young men led to the rise of many of the liquor laws of the state that are largely still in place to this day.

When it came time to actually send men and women overseas, New Jersey responded as willingly as any other state in the nation. In all, some 130,000 of its residents volunteered or were drafted for World War I. While some units had been mustered into service in June 1916, these men were mostly released by October. It wouldn't be until August 5, 1917, that the 1st New Jersey Regiment was organized at Sea Girt. Other formations followed, and on October 11, the 1st, 4th and 7th New Jersey were consolidated by the federal government into the 113th Regiment as part of the 29th Division. Likewise, the 1st New Jersey Cavalry squadron, which had formed in Newark on May 29, 1913, was mustered into federal service in late July 1917 before being broken up two months later and parceled out to various other military police and artillery units. The New Jersey National Guard itself was sent to Camp McClellan in Alabama for ten months of training before departing for France.

New Jersey's sons once again fought honorably in all major battles of the war. After arriving in France in June 1918, men and units from the state were present at the Meuse-Argonne as well as at various battles in Alsace and Lorraine. Among these many soldiers was Harold G. Hoffman, future governor of the state and who was famously connected to the Lindbergh Trial. Another important resident was Private Needham Roberts of Trenton, a member of the famed 369th Infantry, better known as the Harlem Hellfighters. Due to his heroic actions on the field, Roberts became one of only two Americans to receive the Croix de Guerre during World War I. Residents of the state received eight Medals of Honor for their actions. Perhaps most notable among them was Captain Louis Miles of the 308th Infantry from Princeton, who led his men in an

Soldiers returning from France to Hoboken aboard the USS *Agamemnon*. *Library of Congress*.

Harlem Hellfighters from New York and New Jersey. *National Archives*.

assault on a position near the Aisne Canal. After being shot five times, he ordered himself to be carried at the front of his regiment on a stretcher in order to still lead his men into battle.

Poet James Lane Pennypacker of New Jersey highlighted the courage of the Jersey Blues in yet another war in one of his many poems, this one written months before any soldier from the Garden State actually saw combat:

> *Mother, dear Mother, thy sons are proclaiming*
> *Loyalty; with their banners aflaming*
> *The Jersey Blues still march at thy side,*
> *Eager to cheer thee with love and with pride,*
> *Ready to guard thee, whatever betide.*
> *New Jersey!*[100]

As the war came to a halt in November 1918, New Jersey changed its roles and became the main demobilization center for the U.S. Army. As millions of American men and women trickled back into Hoboken, Governor Edge again attempted proactive action to help the returning residents of his state. A plan by the governor was crafted to aid in the rehabilitation and reintegration of soldiers into civilian life. The legislation envisioned a massive public works program to provide jobs for unemployed veterans, the making available of education to help train the men for the workforce and the establishment of clinics to help battle the numerous cases of venereal disease that plagued the army. Though the assembly did not act on Edge's proposal, his ideas would later be incorporated into various pieces of federal legislation before and after World War II. The governor himself would go on to serve as a senator from the state of New Jersey from 1919 to 1929. During his time in Washington, Edge's most important vote was undoubtedly on the nation's approval of the Treaty of Versailles. Though a moderate Republican, the former governor voted for the Lodge Reservations in order to maintain American independence in foreign affairs. Edge's vote helped to ensure the failure of ratification and kept the United States out of the League of Nations.

New Jersey's experience with the Great War was overshadowed by one of the deadliest diseases of the century. The last year of the war saw the outbreak of Spanish influenza, a disease that would kill more people around the planet than the conflict itself. It has long been a matter of debate as to where the contagion originated, and despite its nomenclature, Spain was not a contender. Most historians agree that the illness sprang up in America, but they are unsure as to whether ground zero was in Kansas or New Jersey. Wartime censorship largely restricted news of the disease from being broadcast in the open, and as the Public Health Service did not require states to report statistics on the number of infected until September 1918, it is difficult to determine when the disease first began to appear in the state. It is assumed that a soldier at Fort Dix who was returning from Europe was patient zero in the state. From him, the contagion quickly spread to other servicemen, nurses and workers on the base and then outward into the community. By September, the state reported to the federal government that the sickness was "unusually prevalent." By October 10, public gatherings were banned, and a week later, around 90,000 confirmed cases were identified in New Jersey. After another week, this number had almost doubled to 150,000. Increased deaths led to drastic actions by local and state leaders. Warehouses were requisitioned to help store the bodies that were piling up, public funerals were banned and mass graves became the norm in most towns. Though the disease tapered off as winter approached, it continued to be present well into the next summer. In the end, the state would see around 4,400 deaths from influenza, while only 3,400 were felled by the bullets of the Germans.

CHAPTER 9

AGAINST THE AXIS: NEW JERSEY IN WORLD WAR II

A generation later, New Jersey was once again at war—this time with both Germany and Japan. Shipyards roared back into action, men and women signed up for service and the factories of the state, long dormant from the Depression, again began to churn out goods and materials. Once again, the state's industry would prove to be its largest contribution to the Allied victory. Although New Jersey was not the same target it had been for the Germans in World War I, a number of important incidents would still take place on its soil.

Incidents of sabotage against the state paled in comparison to those from the Great War. The earliest and most deadly of these was the Hercules Powder Plant Disaster of 1940. Located in Kenvil in Roxbury, the Hercules Plant, an offshoot of DuPont, helped to produce explosives for the Allies during World War II. The massive complex covered 1,200 acres and was already mass-producing weapons well before America's entrance into the conflict. At 1:30 p.m. on September 12, an explosion detonated the 297,000 pounds of gunpowder stored in and around the plant. At least twenty buildings were leveled, and the shockwave was recorded on seismographic equipment at Fordham University in New York City. It is estimated that around fifty-two were killed and over one hundred injured in the blast and subsequent fire along with millions of dollars' worth of damage.

It was unclear both at the time and for years afterward who was responsible for the disaster. While some blamed the blast on an industrial accident, others were quick to point fingers at Nazi sabotage. Karl Franz Rekowski, a German spy in the area, alleged that an IRA group had carried out the attack in order to weaken the British. Various attempts during the war at collaboration between the Nazis and the IRA had occurred prior to this event and would continue (though producing little result) until almost the end of the war. A final party blamed for the attack was the group of German Americans residing in the state, specifically those living around Sussex County.

In the 1930s, New Jersey and New York were home to the largest and most active chapters of the German American Bund. A pro-Nazi organization, the Bund trained youth, spread propaganda and sought to help and push Nazi policy by any means necessary. Fear of the group and the violence that was often associated with its rallies led Assemblymen John Rafferty of Middlesex and Samuel Pesin of Jersey City in 1934 to propose legislation aimed at outlawing the Bund. However, thanks to efforts by the ACLU and others, this bill died in committee. Further meetings and riots occurred in Newark and Irvington until 1935, when Rafferty re-proposed and was able to push through a bill outlawing the type of hate speech practiced by the various pro-Nazi groups in the state. By 1938, Congress, too, was investigating such subversive groups as the German American Bund, with Congressman Samuel Dickstein pointing out disdainfully the opening of Camp Nordland in Andover, Sussex County, only a week before. An investigation by Congress revealed that the camp was located near an ammunition dump and powder mill and that its *bundesfuhrer*, Fritz Julius Kuhn, had received support from New Jersey state senator William Dolan. Thousands would attend rallies at the camp, while hundreds of children were sent there by their parents for summer activities that often amounted to paramilitary training. Other camps soon sprang up in New Jersey and New York, including Camp Bergwald at Federal Hill in Bloomingdale, the site of the Pompton Mutiny of 1781. By 1939, as the riots and disorders associated with the group increased, the state passed additional measures aimed at weakening the Bund. Some of these laws included making it illegal to appear in public in the uniform of a foreign military, increased fees for the licensing of shooting ranges like the one at Nordland and the refusal to renew the club's liquor license. The downfall of Nordland quickened with the arrest and conviction of Kuhn on charges of embezzlement in 1939. More arrests were made following the Hercules Explosion in 1940. Though the New Jersey Supreme Court struck down Rafferty's law on December 5,

1941, on the grounds that it violated both the state constitution as well as the Fourteenth Amendment, the days of the New Jersey Bund were over.

A similar group operated out of Union County under the leadership of Dr. Salvatore Caridi. Composed of Italian veterans from World War I and fascists, Caridi's Blackshirts worked closely with the Bund. Caridi himself gave a well-received speech during the opening ceremony for Camp Nordland, recommending "a punch in the nose" for those who demonized Hitler or Mussolini yet at the same time denying links between his organization and the Nazi Party.[101]

Nazi Germany itself attempted only two other major instances of sabotage against the United States. In 1941, thanks to a double agent among its ranks, the FBI was able to arrest and convict the thirty-three members of the Duquesne Spy Ring. This group was composed of German immigrants who were placed in various industrial, transportation and military positions throughout America. Their goal was to sabotage the war fighting and production ability of the nation once war was declared. One of its members, Carl Reuper, worked at Westinghouse Electric in Newark and ran a splinter cell of agents who sought to steal technological secrets. The FBI was able to string Reuper along for months, supplying him with worthless technological blueprints in order to identify more members of the spy ring. In the end, the government was able to arrest Reuper and a co-conspirator named Paul Fehse, who was attempting to sail from Hoboken to Lisbon, as well as dozens of other conspirators in other states.

The following year, a final attempt by Hitler to subvert American industry, Operation Pastorius, was defeated as well. Modeled after the Black Tom Island incident, eight German agents landed on the edge of Long Island and Florida in June 1942. The initial plan called for a landing at one of three locations: Seaside Park, Ocean City or Long Island. The latter of these was eventually chosen as providing the least chance of detection. Fortunately, the group was quickly discovered and rounded up within weeks. Among their list of targets disclosed during the investigation was Pennsylvania Station in Newark. Again, New Jersey was a prime target for the Führer.

In fact, the dangers of industrial sabotage were perennially on the minds of leaders in the state. In April 1943, the SS *El Estero*, loaded with 1,365 tons of munitions, caught fire while moored in Bayonne. As the fire raged, fears grew over the condition of the estimated 5,000 tons of munitions stored around the docks. Firefighters eventually dragged the boat deeper into the river and sank it in order to prevent the volatile cargo on board from exploding. Federal and state officials began to devise an alternative to storing ammunition in populated areas in such a potentially dangerous way. The result was the construction of Naval Weapons Station Earle beginning in August 1943. Located on a spit of land jutting into Sandy Hook Bay, it was far enough away from major urban areas to reduce the risk of a repeat of Black Tom Island.

Thanks to its use of a convoy system and various other countermeasures, the coast of New Jersey was able to largely avoid the depredations usually brought upon it during war by enemy warships. Yet numerous sinkings did still take place, especially during Operation Drumbeat, in which *U-123* sank a series of vessels up and down the Atlantic coast, most notably the *Coimbra* on January 15, 1942, off Sandy Hook. The most notable loss was the destroyer USS *Jacob Jones*, which had been built by New York Shipbuilding in Camden in 1918. While patrolling near Cape May in 1942, the ship spotted the still-burning remains of the *R.P. Resor*, which had been torpedoed off Barnegat the day before. On the following day, February 28, *Jacob Jones* was torpedoed by the same German submarine that had sunk the merchantman. Two torpedoes struck the destroyer and sealed its fate. Only 11 men out of the crew of 113 were rescued from the ship and brought safely to Cape May. *Jones* represented the first American warship lost in combat in home waters during the war. Many shore towns, reluctant to lose income during the war, refused to dim their lights at night, creating an ideal environment for the few U-boats that made it to the coast. In such a crowded sea-lane, numerous accidental sinkings were bound to occur as well. Two of the more notable were the October 16, 1943 loss of the USS *Moonstone*, which collided with the USS *Greer*, and the USS *St. Augustine*, which sank on January 6, 1944. Both wrecks lie off Cape May.[102]

Once again, the state served as a training and embarkation point for the millions of men being transported to Europe to fight against the Axis. Camp Dix, renamed Fort Dix in 1939, saw ten divisions pass through its basic training program before departing for Europe. Farther north, Camp Kilmer was established in 1942 in Piscataway. The facility was named for New Brunswick resident Joyce Kilmer, author of the often-parodied poem "Trees," who had fallen at the Second Battle of the Marne in 1918. Kilmer was built by thousands of workers and contained, among other things, seven chapels, five theaters, nine post offices, twenty baseball fields and three libraries. Around twenty divisions would move through Kilmer on their way to war, twice the number of Fort Dix. Processing about 2.5 million men, the camp was the largest single embarkation point in the nation during the war.

Numerous air bases and training facilities were established by the U.S. Army Air Corps in the state as well. Notable among these was Linden Airport, next to which was a GM plant that produced the airplanes flown from the field and where the navy operated a blimp base, less than fifty miles from the site of the crash of the famed *Hindenburg* in 1937. Modern-day Newark-Liberty Airport was also operated by the army during the war and famously received advanced German aircraft seized as part of Operation Lusty and transported to America aboard the HMS *Reaper* in 1945. Naval Air Station Wildwood, originally known as Rio Grande, was established in 1943 and helped to train pilots for dive-bombing missions. Over the course of the war, Wildwood would see over 129 crashes and 42 deaths in training. Millville Army Airfield, which housed the First Air Force, became known as "America's First Defense Airport." Started in August 1941, four months before the nation was at war, the facility would eventually train over 1,200 pilots from 1943 to 1945. After the war, Millville was used as a housing facility for returning veterans to help them transition back to civilian life.

To help protect the state and region, the U.S. Army both updated existing facilities and began construction on new defenses throughout New Jersey. Lookout towers, some as tall as six stories, were constructed along the coast of the state to help scan the ocean for U-boats. Most have been dismantled over the years, but one tower still stands in Cape May. The latter location also became the site of the construction of a small gun emplacement that likewise remains to this day. Built between 1941 and 1942, it housed four 155mm coastal guns as well as a collection of six-inch guns. The bastion was meant to complement Fort Miles, which stood across the bay at Lewes, Delaware, guarding the approaches to the Delaware Bay and River.

As always, the industrial strength of New Jersey proved to be one of its most conspicuous contributions to the war effort. One of the successful endeavors occurred at the General Motors plant in Linden. Between 1937 and 1941, this factory had produced a third of a million automobiles for consumers and could eject a completed car from the factory in sixty seconds. Unfortunately, the advent of war had threatened to shutter its doors. Executives from the plant traveled to Washington in an attempt to gain a government contract and save thousands of jobs. The result was a partnership with Grumman out of Long Island that produced a brand-new division, Eastern Aircraft. The Linden Division, along with the Delco-Remy battery plant in Bloomfield and the Trenton-Ternsteldt Plant in Trenton, would join this new enterprise in 1942. Over the course of the war, they would produce over seven thousand F4F Wildcats and almost ten thousand Grumman TBF Avengers, including the one piloted by future president George H.W. Bush. These represented the vast majority of those particular aircraft built in the nation. Other facilities across the state included the Curtiss-Wright plant in Paterson, which produced thousands of airplane engines during the war, including those of the *Enola Gay*. This factory also helped to produce the P-40 Warhawk, the C-46 Transport, the SB2C Helldiver, the A-25 Helldiver and the P-47 Republic Thunderbolt. Similar plants owned by Lockheed Martin and others existed in Camden and Cherry Hill. Additional industries of the state helped to produce materials for the Manhattan Project, including Westinghouse in Bloomfield, which focused on the production of uranium.

The state's shipyards also sprang into action in 1941. New York Shipbuilding in Camden turned out vessels continuously during the war. Receiving a $20 million grant from the federal government, it expanded its operations and eventually employed over thirty thousand men and women. Various ships were constructed in its berths, including the battleship *South Dakota*, heavy cruisers *Alaska* and *Hawaii*, various light aircraft carriers and 148 landing craft. Prior to the war, the shipyard had turned out dozens of other ships that would go on to achieve fame in the conflict. Most notable among these were the carrier USS *Saratoga* and the destroyer *Reuben James*, which became the first American warship sunk during the war. Two Camden-built warships, the *Utah* and the *Oklahoma*, were sunk during the attack on Pearl Harbor. Another company, Federal Shipbuilding and Drydock in Kearny, would build more destroyers than any other location in America, save for the famed shipbuilding facility at Bath, Maine. Its record-breaking build of the USS *Melvin* took 103 days from the laying down of the keel until its launch. Federal also opened a facility in Newark in 1942 that, over the course of the war, would build twelve destroyers and fifty-two destroyer escorts.

Being once again used as a main embarkation point for the transport of troops to Europe, New Jersey likewise became an active location for the internment of prisoners flowing back from the battlefield. A variety of camps were set up throughout the state to handle both German and

This General Motors plant in Linden, New Jersey, produced P-47 Thunderbolts during World War II. *National Archives.*

Italian POWs. Among these were the Belle Mead Depot, Fort Dix, the Jersey City Quartermaster Supply Depot, the Raritan Arsenal, Centerton, Parvin State Park in Vineland, Caven Point Jersey City, Fort Monmouth and Port Johnson in Bayonne. At the latter, several hundred Italians were interned and, after the fall of Italy, used for manual labor. Local Italian American families brought home cooked dinners to the prisoners on Sundays, while small groups were even taken on sightseeing tours of New York City. The phenomenal treatment of the prisoners soon became a sore point for many in the state, with the head of the Bayonne Post of the American Legion holding a meeting with the mayor of Bayonne to address grievances.

Seabrook Farms in Upper Deerfield, Cumberland County, played an interesting role regarding prisoners of war in World War II. Before the war, the company was already one of the premier suppliers of produce in the nation, being not only a major supplier to the army but also producing around 20 percent of the country's frozen food. C.F. Seabrook was considered by many at the time to be the Henry Ford of agriculture, utilizing the latest technological innovations and planning to produce food. Once war broke out, the farms of Seabrook needed to supplement their lost labor force; German POWs from nearby camps combined with displaced refugees to fill the ranks of departed Americans. Over thirty-two ethnicities would eventually be represented on the farms and in the factories of the company. Perhaps most interesting was the arrival of 2,500 Japanese Americans who had been held in internment camps in the West under orders from President Roosevelt. Their presence represented one of the largest concentrations of Japanese Americans in the nation at the time.

Women of New Jersey also contributed immensely to the war effort, just as they had consistently done in the past. Besides the most obvious examples or working in factories and tending to victory gardens, several prominent women in the state did their part in the armed forces as well. Colonel Ruth Cheney Streeter of Morristown became the first director of the USMC Women's Reserve in 1943. She would remain in charge of this group until the end of the war. Joy Bright Hancock of Cape May County, who had served in the navy in World War I, was likewise appointed head of the WAVES in 1946. An additional ten thousand women from New Jersey served in both units as well.

Obviously, the largest and most costly contribution by the state came in terms of the number of men it sent to battle overseas. Citizens of New Jersey fought in all major theaters and campaigns of the war, distinguishing themselves as did the Jersey Blues of the past. An estimated 500,000 men from the state enlisted or were drafted into combat over the course of the war. Around 12,500 of these soldiers would make the ultimate sacrifice, making World War II by far the deadliest war for the state in terms of lives lost in combat.

Though soldiers from the state served in various divisions during the war, the 44th Division, composed of the National Guard of both New York and New Jersey, became the most recognizable unit of the state. The division spent most of 1940–44 stateside in various training maneuvers before finally landing in France in September 1944. From October 1944 until March 1945, the 44th slowly pushed forward until it crossed the Rhine at Worms. The unit continued to march through southern Germany before crossing into Austria days before the surrender of the Nazis. While in this area, soldiers from the 44th helped to capture

A New Jersey Coast Guard horse patrol unit during World War II. *National Archives.*

Naval Air Station Lakehurst, site of the Hindenburg crash, under construction in 1943. *National Archives.*

Magnus von Braun, the brother of Wernher von Braun, both of whose work after the war helped to push forward the American missile and space programs. Exemplifying the division's skill and courage during its time in Europe, one soldier of the 44th received the Medal of Honor; fifteen other residents of the state would also be awarded that honor while serving in other units and branches. One unit of the 44th, the 102nd Cavalry, achieved some level of fame by being the first cavalry unit to arrive in England, the first unit to enter Paris, the first to cross the Meuse and the first to collide with the Siegfried Line. One of its members, Sergeant Curtis Cullin, designed the Rhino Plow, which, when attached to the tanks present in Normandy, helped the Allies to break through the hedgerows of the countryside.

Many other notable residents of the state served during the war. Some of the more famous include Admiral William "Bull" Halsey of Elizabeth, who helped to lead the U.S. Navy in the Pacific; Lieutenant John Bulkeley of Hackettstown, who commanded the force that evacuated General Douglas MacArthur from the Philippines; and Gunnery Sergeant John Basilone of Raritan, who received a Medal of Honor for his actions at Guadalcanal. One of New Jersey's many soldiers, Frank Lautenberg, would go on to become the last surviving World War II veteran serving in the U.S. Senate.

Another important individual from the state was Walter Evans Edge. The World War I–era governor was reelected to head the state in 1943. Serving from 1944 to 1947, he again helped to direct the state of New Jersey through both the war and its aftermath. Prior to this, Edge had served as secretary of the navy in 1940. His most notable accomplishment in this position was approving the construction of the *Iowa* class of battleships, naming the second one, the USS *New Jersey*, after his home state.

CHAPTER 10

COLD WAR ALONG THE HOT SHORE: NEW JERSEY AND THE WARS OF MODERNITY

The ending of World War II began a much more dangerous period for America in terms of its foreign affairs. The Cold War would test the nation's resolve for almost half a century. Wars, assassinations, riots and the ever-present specter of nuclear holocaust hung not only over the United States but also New Jersey. The state would again experience all of the wars and challenges of the nation on a microcosmic level. Following the fall of the USSR, the state would see little reprieve from death and destruction as the specter of Islamic terrorism quickly descended upon its cities.

THE COLD WAR

Early on, the state was involved in a rather notorious episode of the Cold War. One of the most famous trials in American history for treason involved Julius and Ethel Rosenberg, who were arrested and executed in 1953 for giving military secrets to the Soviets. From 1940 to 1945, Julius Rosenberg was employed at Fort Monmouth as an engineer. Here he had access to research, diagrams and technology that would be very valuable to the USSR. Rosenberg was eventually fired from his job in 1945 after it was discovered that he had been active in the past in the Communist

Party of America. His brief employment at the fort allowed him to set up a spy ring that included at least two other scientists, who would eventually flee to the Soviet Union after the FBI began to investigate.

On the federal level, concerns over the presence of other communist spies in the nation led to the infamous McCarthy hearings and McCarran Subcommittee. In New Jersey, with its long history of internal subversion, similar concerns prompted action from the state legislature. On March 11, 1947, the New Jersey Assembly passed Concurrent Resolution Number 11 requesting that the governor form a committee to investigate communist and un-American acts and teachings in the state. Two Rutgers professors were called before the McCarran Subcommittee in 1952. Both men, Simon Heimlich and Moses Finley, pleaded the First and Fifth Amendments to questions regarding their communist affiliations. Despite a protest by two hundred people who drove from Newark to New Brunswick, Rutgers decided to fire both professors in December 1952. Yet at the same time, the university hosted a series of lectures by Earl Browder, who headed the Communist Party USA from 1930 to 1945.

The state began its most massive peacetime buildup in order to engage in the Cold War. Fort Dix Army Airbase was reopened in 1948 and renamed McGuire Air Force Base. Its namesake, Thomas McGuire, was born in Ridgewood and, before being killed in combat in 1945, was the second-highest-scoring ace of the war. By 1950, McGuire was the largest military airport in the world. Nearby, Lakehurst Naval Air Station flew blimp patrols that scouted the East Coast for Russian subs. At the same time, New York Shipbuilding of Camden continued to turn out vessels for the navy. Among these were the carrier *Kitty Hawk*, the frigate *Norfolk*, four attack subs, several guided missile cruisers and guided missile destroyers and the nuclear-powered cargo ship *Savannah*.

One of the largest military undertakings in the state was the construction of a series of Nike batteries. New Jersey–based Bell Labs had created the concept in 1945 of a system of antiaircraft missiles that could be based around major America cities to protect them from Soviet bombers and jets. Due to its geography, the state was assured to have numerous such Nike sites constructed on its soil. A ring of antiaircraft guns had already been established in Newark, Paterson, Sandy Hook, Fort Lee and Elizabeth, among other cities, at the height of World War II.

However, the advent of jet engines had rendered the weapons largely outdated. Thus, in 1954, construction began on a ring of defenses

Artillery crew at Fort Hancock, Sandy Hook. *National Park Service.*

around both New York and Philadelphia. The New York defenses were commanded by a headquarters at Atlantic Highlands and based around radar stations built at South Amboy and Morristown. The Nike batteries themselves were located at Middletown, Holmdel, Fort Hancock, Old Bridge, South Plainfield, Summit, Livingston, Wayne and Franklin Lakes. The Philadelphia defenses were headquartered at Pedricktown and controlled batteries at Lumberton, Marlton, Berlin, Pitman and Swedesboro. Though the system was never fired in anger, Battery NY53 in Middletown suffered an accident on May 22, 1958, in which several missiles accidentally detonated, killing ten soldiers and civilians. The nuclear-tipped CIM-10 Bomarc that was slated to replace the Nike system was also first installed at McGuire in 1959. Only nine months later, a fire broke out in one of the missile silos, melting the warhead and spreading nuclear contamination around the site that persists to the present day. In a similar vein, on July 28, 1957, a C-124 Globemaster transporting three nuclear bombs from Delaware to Europe lost power and jettisoned two

Nike missile installation at Sandy Hook. *National Park Service.*

of the bombs off Cape May. The atomic weapons were never recovered and are assumed to still be at the bottom of the ocean.

The first major conflict of the Cold War flared up not in Europe, as was assumed, but in Asia with the Korean Conflict. Various New Jersey National Guard units were federalized during the Korean War. Included among these were the 108th Fighter Wing, the 112th Artillery Group HQ, the 695th Armored Field Artillery Battalion, the 30th Ordinance Battalion, the 63rd Army Band and the 150th Engineer Pontoon Bridge Company. In addition, the 21st Infantry Battalion of the USMC Reserves based out of Dover was also federalized and contributed many fine marines to the war, including a Medal of Honor recipient. Overall, 191,000 men from the state would serve in the war, while 4 residents would receive the nation's highest honor. In the end, an estimated 836 would die or go missing during the largely forgotten conflict.[103]

The advent of the 1960s saw further conflict erupt between the United States and the USSR, much of which again involved New Jersey. In late 1961, at the height of the Berlin Crisis, the 108th Fighter Wing was again activated by the federal government and called to Europe. The 119th Tactical Fighter Squadron from Atlantic City and the 141st Tactical Fighter Squadron from McGuire were sent to Chaumont-Semoutiers in France and remained there until October 1962. This same unit received F-105B Thunderchiefs in April 1964, making it the first Air National Guard unit in the nation to be able to fly twice the speed of sound.

In early October 1962, just before the Cuban Missile Crisis, Roberto Casanova arrived in New York City. He was a Cuban agent dispatched by Castro to wage a campaign of terrorism against America. Among his targets were various landmarks in Manhattan and a list of much more strategic targets in New Jersey. Included among the latter were oil refineries along the Jersey shore and the Humble Oil Refining Company in Linden. Luckily for the nation, the FBI was able to break up the group shortly before the standoff with the USSR later that month.

The Cuban Missile Crisis bears two interesting footnotes that concern the Garden State. On October 28, the last day of the confrontation and one that almost led to a nuclear exchange, a radar facility in Moorestown suddenly detected a launch from Cuba. Base personnel quickly notified NORAD at around 9:00 a.m. that a nuclear missile had taken off from the Caribbean island and was projected to strike in Florida by 9:02 a.m. After a detonation was not reported, officials quickly ascertained that a test tape had been running in the computers of the New Jersey facility. A few months later, in February 1963, much of America was watching the nightly news to witness a presentation by the government on the withdrawal of missiles from Cuba. The man chosen to deliver that information was New Jersey's own John T. Hughes. A graduate of the College of New Jersey, Hughes had been handpicked by the Kennedy administration to deliver the hour-long address to the population of the free world detailing what had happened in Cuba and to reassure the world that disaster had been averted.

Vietnam had earlier connections to New Jersey than perhaps any other state. Seeking to escape assassination attempts in Vietnam, Ngo Dinh Diem lived in exile at Maryknoll Seminary in Lakewood, New Jersey. For three years, Ngo lived in the region and helped to garner money and moral and political support for the cause of freedom in his home country. Following the Geneva Accords, he would return to a divided Vietnam and become prime minister of the south. After his rise to power, Ngo returned to America on a carefully orchestrated state visit in 1957.

Besides the usual accolades from Congress and required pilgrimage to New York City, Ngo traveled to South Orange, where he received an honorary degree from Seton Hall University. During his sojourn in this state during the early 1950s, he had done much to help create the Asian Studies Department of that school, a program that would go on to achieve renown over the next few decades. Diem himself described its role in helping "to salvage what must be salvaged of the values of Asia in the tornado that befell this large portion of the world."[104]

The expansion of the war in Vietnam brought back an age-old conflict in New Jersey. As the history of the state has shown, opposition to war is nothing new to the Garden State. From the anti-war stance of the Quakers in the eighteenth century to dogged Federalist opposition to the War of 1812, dissent has a long history here. Therefore, though some 212,000 residents volunteered or were drafted into service in Southeast Asia, and around 1,556 gave their lives, not all in the state were dedicated to the war. In April 1965, only months after the Gulf of Tonkin Incident, Rutgers University hosted one of the first teach-ins in the nation. Professor Eugene Genovese famously exclaimed, "I do not fear or regret the impending Viet Cong victory in Vietnam. I welcome it."[105] His statements even became one of the issues in the gubernatorial race that year, with Republican candidate Senator Wayne Dumont demanding his removal and current governor Richard J. Hughes opposing his termination. A third teach-in in October of that year, organized by Students for a Democratic Society (SDS), even saw the outbreak of a fight between an anti-war protestor and the mother of a soldier.

At the height of the war in 1969, a number of colleges in the state participated in the nationwide Moratorium to End the War in Vietnam. Rutgers University, Montclair State University, William Paterson College, Jersey City State College and Essex County College all saw mass walkouts, protests, demonstrations and acts of civil disobedience. The *Newark Sunday News* reported, "New Jersey college students with public officials and high school students will march, pray, and sing in protest of Vietnam…a majority of 100,000 students from 56 colleges in New Jersey are expected to participate."[106] Two years later, in August 1971, the Camden 28, a group of nuns, priests and laypeople, raided the draft office in Camden to both protest the war and destroy draft records. Though betrayed by an informant to the FBI, the members of the group were all proclaimed not guilty in a classic example of jury nullification. A more violent incident involved the planned bombing of Fort Dix by the Weathermen in 1970.

Inside the convention hall of Atlantic City during the 1964 Democratic National Convention. *Courtesy of the LBJ Library.*

Only the accidental explosion of the bomb in Greenwich Village, killing three members of the terrorist group, prevented the attack.

Perhaps the most controversial of the protests occurred under the guise of the Vietnam Vets Against the War. As part of Operation RAW, 150 veterans began a uniformed march from Morristown to Valley Forge to demand an immediate end to the war. The protest, which began on September 7, 1970, also involved the portrayal of search-and-destroy missions. Groups of veterans would round up citizens from the various suburbs they marched through in a mock execution of a typical army operation in South Vietnam. Afterward, flyers were then handed out describing the rape, torture and murder that normally would have accompanied such a mission. The end of the march saw speeches from such notables as John Kerry, Jane Fonda, George McGovern and Ed Muskie.

In an effort to bring about an end to the conflict in Vietnam and ease tensions between East and West, President Johnson agreed to a summit with the Soviet premier, Alexei Kosygin. Disagreement over whether to hold the conference in New York City or Washington, combined with fears of growing protest movements disrupting the talks, led to the summit being held at Glassboro State College, now Rowan University. The two men met and talked from June 23 to June 25 in 1967, with topics ranging from concerns over the conflict currently raging in the Middle East to the war in Vietnam. Though no lasting peace was established, the "Spirit of Glassboro" that pervaded the talks was seen as a thawing of the animosity between the United States and the USSR.

Other issues, though, surfaced as more important to the residents of New Jersey's cities in the 1960s. Race riots erupted in Jersey City, Paterson and Elizabeth in 1964. In July 1967, massive riots erupted in both Newark and Plainfield over issues of poverty and lack of progress in civil rights. In Newark alone, twenty-six people were killed and over seven hundred wounded. The National Guard was called in to restore order and patrolled the streets for days. At the same time, the rioters in Plainfield broke into the Plainfield Machine Company and stole forty-six M1 carbines. Around three hundred police and National Guardsmen would search house to house without warrants to recover the stolen weapons. More National Guard troops had to be brought in using armored personal carriers to relieve the besieged fire department station. Order was not restored in either town until almost the end of the month, with the economic and social damage lasting for decades. Similar riots erupted in 1970 in Asbury Park and in Camden in 1971.

New Jersey's experiences at war continued even as the Cold War approached its end. Perhaps the most fitting instrument of military strategy in all major actions of the war was the USS *New Jersey* itself. The huge battleship participated with honor in World War II, Korea and Vietnam. As the 1980s dawned, the ship was again commissioned as part of Reagan's expansion of the navy and called back into service at various points. In 1983, it was dispatched to Lebanon to help monitor the situation during the civil war there. To help relieve pressure on U.S. Marines in Beirut, the *New Jersey* fired its main guns at entrenched rebels. This represented the first use of sixteen-inch shells in combat anywhere on the planet since the ship had last fired its guns in anger in Vietnam in 1969. In 1986, the *New Jersey* sailed through the Sea of Okhotsk, representing the first time that an American battleship had ever sailed through Russian territorial waters. The ship was finally decommissioned for the last time in 1991 as the Cold War was ending. Having served from 1943 to 1991, the ship's lifetime overlapped America's confrontation of the USSR.

In the immediate aftermath of the Cold War, New Jersey continued to participate in the wars of the nation in the 1990s. During the buildup to the Persian Gulf War, three National Guard units from the state were called up, over seven hundred men in total, to help support Operation Desert Shield. Included among these was the 108th Air Refueling Wing, which proved to be vital to the successful air war over Iraq. Perhaps New Jersey's greatest contribution to the war, though, was General "Stormin'" Norman Schwarzkopf. Born in Trenton and the son of the first superintendent of the New Jersey State Police, Schwarzkopf had served with honor in Vietnam and helped to lead the invasion of Grenada in the 1980s.[107] His preparations and careful planning allowed for a quick and complete victory in the war, much as New Jersey resident General Scott had done in Mexico back in the 1840s. Eight soldiers from New Jersey would die during the short campaign. Two others, Jeffrey Zaun of Cherry Hill and Robert Wentzel of Metuchen, were shot down and held by the Iraqis for six weeks. Images of them as POWs would be seen throughout America, thanks to CNN's televised coverage of the war.

The state was also represented in the final major campaign of the twentieth century. During Operation Noble Anvil, the NATO bombing of Serbia during the Kosovo War, various New Jersey units again took part. The 108th Air Refueling Wing and the 107th Fighter Wing were once more activated and brought to Europe to help achieve peace. At the same time, McGuire Air Force Base was selected as one of the major sites to house Kosovo refugees during the conflict. Thousands of displaced people would be housed in New Jersey during the conflict as part of an effort to relocate an estimated twenty thousand to the United States. Many of these ethnic Albanians would settle in the state after the war ended.

TERRORISM

The wave of terror attacks that struck the United States at the end of the twentieth century had a direct impact on the state of New Jersey. Attacks were planned on its soil, terrorists lived in its cities undetected and many residents of the state died as a result of the assaults. Once America began to strike back, residents of the state responded as earnestly as they had in any previous conflict.

The particular philosophy of militant, extremist Islam that became associated with the various attacks of 9/11 and Al Qaeda first arrived in

New Jersey in the early 1990s. One of the leaders of this movement in the state was Sheik Omar Abdel-Rahman, better known as the Blind Sheik. Having been involved with various Egyptian terrorist groups in the 1970s and with Osama bin Laden in the 1980s, Abdel-Rahman arrived in America in 1990 on a tourist visa. He became a spiritual advisor to many of the terrorists living in New Jersey and New York while preaching at the Al Salam Mosque in Jersey City. Some of his most notable followers were Ali Mohamed, who stole intelligence and manuals from Fort Bragg, and El Sayyid Nosair of Cliffside Park, who killed Rabbi Meir Kahane in 1990.

One of the most notable attacks planned by followers of the Blind Sheik was the 1993 World Trade Center bombing. Spearheaded by Ramzi Yousef of Jersey City, the attack called for the use of a 1,500-pound bomb to cripple the foundation of the World Trade Center in New York City. When the attack failed to achieve its desired goal, Abdel-Rahman encouraged the follow-up New York City Landmark Bombing Plot, which would have destroyed various bridges, tunnels and landmarks around the city, including the United Nations Headquarters. Luckily, the attack was foiled, with Yousef fleeing the nation and the Blind Sheik being arrested. In 1995, Abdel-Rahman was convicted of seditious conspiracy and sentenced to life in prison.

The failure of militant Muslims to successfully attack the United States in the early 1990s led to the larger 9/11 attacks of 2001. One of the airplanes targeted by Al Qaeda, American Airlines Flight 93, took off from Newark, and while its intended target was in Washington, the passengers managed to fight for control of the plane, causing it to crash in Shanksville, saving possibly hundreds of lives. New Jersey suffered the second-most casualties of any state from the attacks, at 714. The city of Hoboken itself lost 39 citizens, the highest of any town in the state. Following the formation of the 9/11 Commission to investigate the attacks, former New Jersey governor Tom Kean was chosen to head the group and deliver its findings.

The subsequent wars in Afghanistan and Iraq again saw thousands from the state enlist to defend their nation. As of 2013, the state has lost 152 of its citizens in these conflicts, including 3 women, with two-thirds of the casualties arising out of the War in Iraq. General Raymond Odierno of Rockaway helped to organize the Surge in Iraq in 2007 and held overall command of allied forces there from 2008 to 2010.

During the War on Terror, the government has reported breaking up numerous plots aimed at further inflicting death and destruction on the nation. Not surprisingly, New Jersey often figures prominently in many of these operations. In August 2004, a terror cell led by Dhiren Barot was broken up in Pakistan while seeking to attack financial targets in New York City and Newark, as well as use a dirty bomb against London. In December of the following year, Michael Reynolds of Pennsylvania was arrested for attempting to contact jihadists and for plotting to blow up the Standard Oil refinery in New Jersey. The train tunnels connecting New Jersey to New York City became the target of an Al-Qaeda allied group led by Assem Hammoud in July 2006. Finally, after a sixteen-month infiltration operation, the FBI arrested six men in May 2007 for plotting to attack Fort Dix. The plan called for an all-out assault on the installation using assault rifles and grenades, with the plotters carrying out training missions in the Poconos. All six were eventually apprehended and sentenced to prison.

From its exploration by Henry Hudson in 1609, two years after the settlement of Jamestown, to the present day, New Jersey has had a long history on the American continent. The military episodes of the colonists who inhabited its soil to the wars fought by the state have ensured it a place of honor in American military history. As has been seen as well over the past few centuries, the Garden State's merchants, farmers, factory workers, women and politicians played an equally important role in defending both New Jersey and the United States. Though wars have become far removed from American soil, thanks to its industry, demographics and geography, New Jersey remains on the front lines of conflict. Again, William Gould perhaps best sums up the demand of those of the state: "Soldiers! The eyes of the world are fixed on our Country; let us prove that we are worthy of our freedom; let every citizen become a Soldier, and every Soldier a Patriot."

NOTES

CHAPTER 1

1. Richard Calmet Adams (1905) as quoted by Adrienne Mayor in *Fossil Legends of the First Americans* (Princeton, NJ: Princeton Press, 2005), 66.
2. Herbert Kraft, *The Lenape* (N.p.: Lenape Books, 2001), 37.
3. See Peter Lindestron's *Geographia Americae* for a firsthand, detailed description of the Susquehanna.
4. George P. Donehoo, *A History of Indian Villages and Place Names in Pennsylvania* (Harrisburg, PA: Telegraph Press, 1928), 131.
5. David de Vries, *Journal*, in Albert Cook Myers, *Narratives of Early Pennsylvania, West New Jersey, and Delaware 1630–1707* (New York: Barnes and Noble Inc., 1959), 24.
6. Kraft, *The Lenape*, 159.
7. Alanson Skinner, *The Indians of Manhattan Island and Vicinity: A Guide to the Special Exhibition at the American Museum of Natural History* (New York: American Museum of Natural History, 1909), 11.
8. Robert Juet, *Journal of the Voyage of the* Half Moon (Newark: New Jersey Historical Society, 1959), 592.
9. Thomas Frost, "The Death of Colman" in Burton Egbert Stevenson, *Poems of American History* (Boston: Houghton Mifflin, 1908), 50.

10. David de Vries, *Voyages from Holland to America 1632–1644* (New York: Billin and Brothers, 1853), 33–34.

11. Ibid., 32.

12. Johan Printz letter, June 11, 1644.

13. Adrian C. Leiby, *The Early Dutch and Swedish Settlers of New Jersey* (Princeton, NJ: D. Van Nostrand Company Inc., 1964), 34.

14. David de Vries as recorded in John Jameson, *Narratives of New Netherlands* (Carlisle, MA: Applewood Books, 2009), 227.

15. Ibid., 228.

16. Ibid., 229.

17. Leiby, *Early Dutch and Swedish Settlers*, 38.

18. Lamberton would eventually die at sea in 1645 while sailing to England. Cotton Mather's notes of seeing a phantom ship afterward were eventually transformed into a Henry Wadsworth Longfellow poem entitled "The Phantom Ship."

19. Leiby, *Early Dutch and Swedish Settlers*, 60.

20. Sources vary as to whether the Dutch themselves or the Lenape burned down Fort Nassau, with the Swedish engineer Lindstrom writing in 1656 claiming the latter.

21. Lindestron, *Geographia Americae*, 259.

22. Ibid., 260.

CHAPTER 2

23. William A. Whitehead, *East Jersey Under the Proprietary Governments* (Newark: New Jersey Historical Society, 1846), 29.

24. Malcolm C. Gilman, *The Story of the Jersey Blues* (Trenton, NJ: Trenton Publishing Company, 1962), 12.

25. Gilman, *Jersey Blues*, 4, as quoted from Liber I of Woodbridge Town Records.

26. *Records of the Town of Newark, New Jersey from 1666–1836* (Newark: New Jersey Historical Society 1864), 75.

27. "Affidavit of M' William Hayes Concerning ye Taking of New York" from *Documents Relating to the Colonial History of New York*, Vol. III (Albany, 1853), 213.

28. Philip Carteret to Edmund Andros, March 20, 1679, in Aaron Leaming, *The Grants and Concessions and Original Constitutions of the Province of New Jersey* (Philadelphia: W. Bradford, printer, 1881), 674.

29. "Excerpts from the Minutes of a Special Court of Assizes, Held in New York, for the Trail of Philip Carteret," in *Documents Relating to the Colonial History of the State of New Jersey*, Vol. I, 1,631–87 (Newark, NJ: Daily Journal Establishment, 1880), 303.

30. Philip Carteret to Mr. Coustrier (1680), in *Documents Relating to the Colonial History of the State of New Jersey*, Vol. I, 1,631–87, 316.

31. *New Jersey Archives*, Vol. III (Newark, NJ: Daily Advertiser Printing House, 1888), 485.

32. George C. Beekman, *Early Dutch Settlers of Monmouth County, New Jersey* (Freehold, NJ: Moreau Brothers Publishers, 1915), 61–62.

33. Ibid., 63–64

34. John Perlin, *A Forest Journey: The Story of Wood and Civilization* (New York: Countryman Press, 2005).

35. Brendan McConville, *These Daring Disturbers of the Public Peace: The Struggle for Property and Power in Early New Jersey* (Philadelphia: University of Pennsylvania Press, 2003), 188.

36. Francis Bazley Lee, *New Jersey as a Colony and as a State* (New York: Publishing Society of New Jersey, 1903), 376.

37. *New York Mercury*, March 3, 1755.

38. Lee, *New Jersey*, 376.

39. *New York Mercury*, June 22, 1756.

40. A December 15, 1755 letter from Easton, Pennsylvania; quoted in Jennie Sweetman, "French and Indian War: A Major Event in Sussex County," *The Herald* (April 2013).

41. William R. Nester, *The First Global War: Britain, France, and the Fate of North America 1756–1775* (Westport, CT: Greenwood Publishing, 2000), 21.

42. Louis Antoine de Bougainville as recorded in David Newton, *They Came from Away: Yanks, Brits, and Cape Breton* (N.p.: iUniverse, 2010), 25.

43. *Boston News Letter*, September 28, 1758.

44. *New York Mercury*, June 5, 1758.

45. Francis Bernard to William Pitt in *New Jersey Archives*, Vol. VIII, Part 2 (Newark, NJ: Daily Advertiser Printing House, 1888), 167.

46. *New York Mercury*, July 1759.

47. Numbers as quoted from Thomas Purvis in Mark Lender, *One State in Arms: A Short Military History of New Jersey* (Trenton: New Jersey Historical Society, 1991).

48. Charles Stickney, *A History of the Minisink Region in Orange County, New York* (Middletown, NY: Coe Finch and I.F. Guiwits, 1867), 51.

Chapter 3

49. Edmund Morgan, ed., *Prologue to Revolution: Sources and Documents on the Stamp Act Crisis 1764–1765* (Chapel Hill: University of North Carolina Press, 1959), 115–16.

50. Charles Clinton Beatty to Enoch Greene, January 31, 1774.

51. James Madison Jr. to James Madison Sr., July 23, 1770, in Ralph Louis Ketcham, *James Madison: A Biography* (Charlottesville: University of Virginia Press, 1971), 37.

52. Mark Lender, "The Cockpit Reconsidered: Revolutionary New Jersey as a Military Theater," in Barbara Mitnick, ed., *New Jersey in the American Revolution* (New Brunswick, NJ: Rutgers University Press, 2005), 58.

53. James McCloy, *The Jersey Devil* (Wallingford, PA: Middle Atlantic Press, 1976), 25.

54. Alfred Bill Hoyt, *New Jersey and the Revolutionary War* (New Brunswick, NJ: Rutgers University Press, 1978), 7.

55. Alexander Papers, 86.

56. Carol Karels, ed., *The Revolutionary War in Bergan County: The Times That Tries Men's Souls* (Charleston, SC: The History Press, 2007), 25.

57. Thomas Paine, *American Crisis*.

58. Ibid.

59. Matthias Williamson to George Washington, December 8, 1776.

60. Benson John Lossing, *The Pictorial Field Book of the Revolution*, Vol. I (New York: Harper & Brothers, 1850), 36.

61. Hoyt, *New Jersey*, 20.

62. Lossing, *Pictorial Field Book*, 36.

63. Legend states that Jonas Cattell ran from Haddonfield to Fort Mercer to warn of Von Donop's approach.

64. George Washington to Robert Howe, January 22, 1781.

65. George Washington to Matthias Ogden, March 28, 1782.

Chapter 4

66. John Doughty to Henry Knox, October 21, 1785, in William Henry Smith, ed., *The St. Clair Papers: The Life and Public Services of Arthur St. Clair* (Freeport, NY: Books for Libraries Press, 1970).

67. Henry Knox to Arthur St. Clair, December 19, 1789, in Carter, *Territorial Papers, Northwest Territory,* 1:224–26.
68. George Washington to the chiefs of the Choctaw Nation, December 17, 1789.
69. Richard Howell to his mother, September 25, 1794.
70. Gilman, *Jersey Blues,* 10.
71. Paul A. Stellhorn, ed., *Governors of New Jersey 1664–1974: Biographical Essays* (Trenton: New Jersey Historical Commission, 1982), 85.
72. James McHenry to Jonathan Dayton, November 19, 1798.
73. Jonathan Dayton to Alexander Hamilton, March 20, 1799.
74. Joseph Bloomfield to Thomas Jefferson, November 10, 1801.
75. *A History of the City of Newark, New Jersey,* Vol. II (New York: Lewis Historical Publishing Co., 1913), 598.
76. James J. Wilson, letter, April 25, 1812.
77. John C. Fredriksen, *The War of 1812 in Person: Fifteen Accounts by United States Army Regulars, Volunteers and Militiamen* (New York: McFarland, 2010), 163.
78. Stellhorn, *Governors of New Jersey,* 88.
79. *A History of the City of Newark,* 597.
80. Edwin Salter, *A History of Monmouth and Ocean Counties, New Jersey* (Bayonne, NJ: E. Gardner & Son, 1890), 290–93.
81. *New York Spectator,* November 28, 1812.
82. *A History of the City of Newark,* 601.

Chapter 5

83. *Trenton News,* October 9, 1847.

Chapter 6

84. *New York Times,* "The Result in New Jersey," November 10, 1860.
85. W. Barksdale Maynard, "Our Forgotten Civil War," *New Jersey Monthly* (March 2011).
86. Brad Tuttle, *How Newark Became Newark: The Rise, Fall, and Rebirth of an American City* (New Brunswick, NJ: Rutgers University Press, 2009), 48.

87. Charles Smith Olden to Samuel Starr, July 1, 1862.
88. Tuttle, *How Newark Became Newark*, 51.
89. Mark R. Wilson, *The Business of Civil War: Military Mobilization and the State, 1861–1865* (Baltimore, MD: Johns Hopkins University Press, 2006), 235.
90. English poet Henry Newbolt immortalized Craven in one of his poems.
91. William J. Jackson, *New Jerseyans in the Civil War: For Union and Liberty* (New Brunswick, NJ: Rutgers University Press, 2000), 56.

Chapter 7

92. *New York Times*, "NEW YORK AND NEW JERSEY: Enlisted Men on the Warship, Those Who Are Saved Being Indicated by Their Condition," February 17, 1898.
93. Ibid., "German Americans Ready," February 28, 1898.
94. *Elizabeth Daily Journal*, June 1927.
95. *New York Times*, "Militia Strength of States," March 17, 1898.
96. Richard Fernicola, *Twelve Days of Terror* (Guilford, CT: Lyons Press, 2001), 7–8.

Chapter 8

97. Franz von Rintelen, *The Dark Invader: Wartime Reminiscences of a German Naval Intelligence Officer* (N.p.: Taylor & Francis, 1998), 67.
98. *New York Times*, "Sharks and Submarines," July 15, 1916.
99. The *Caroline* had previously been chartered by the government for use as a transport during the Spanish-American War.
100. James Lane Pennypacker, June 2, 1917.

Chapter 9

101. Investigation of Un-American Activities and Propaganda. Report of the Special Committee on Un-American Activities (January 3, 1939), 110.

102. The USS *Greer* was famous for being the first ship fired on by the Germans months before the start of the war.

CHAPTER 10

103. Figures are from the National Archives. The New Jersey Korean War Memorial estimates that the actual number is closer to 890.
104. James T. Fisher, "The Vietnam Lobby and the Politics of Pluralism," in Christian G. Appy, *Cold War Constructions: The Political Culture of United States Imperialism, 1945–1966* (Amherst: University of Massachusetts Press, 2000), 228.
105. Dorothy Ansart, "Inventory to the Records of the Office of Public Information on the Vietnam War Teach-ins, 1965–1966," Special Collections and University Archives, Rutgers University Libraries, RG 07/A2/01.
106. *Newark Sunday News*, October 12, 1969.
107. Schwarzkopf's father, Major General Herbert N. Schwarzkopf, helped lead the CIA operation to install the shah in Iran in 1953.

INDEX

A

Alexander, William (Lord Stirling) 71, 73
Al Qaeda 175, 176
Andros, Edmund 36, 37, 38, 40
Asgill Affair 89
Atlantic Highlands 47

B

Bainbridge, William 100
Baldwin, Samuel 49
Batsto Village 68, 77, 104
Battle of Bad Axe 110
Battle of Bull Run 121
Battle of Cartagena de Indias 45
Battle of Chantilly 122
Battle of Chestnut Neck 68
Battle of Connecticut Farms 86
Battle of Cooks Mill 107
Battle of Fallen Timbers 95
Battle of Fort George 107
Battle of Fort Mifflin 85
Battle of Fort Ticonderoga 60
Battle of Fredericksburg 124
Battle of Gaines' Mill 122
Battle of Gettysburg 124

Battle of Havana 61
Battle of Long Island 73
Battle of Louisbourg 46
Battle of Meuse-Argonne 152
Battle of Monmouth 86
Battle of New Bern 122
Battle of Paulus Hook 86
Battle of Princeton 82
Battle of Roanoke 121
Battle of Sabbath Day Point 57
Battle of Springfield 86
Battle of the Lacolle River 106
Battle of the Wabash 94
Battle of Turtle Gut Inlet 69
Battle of York 106
Battles of Bound Brook 84
Bayonne 159, 163
Black Hawk War 109
Black Sunday 149
Black Tom Island Explosion 145, 147,
    159, 160
Bloomfield, Joseph 90, 100, 102,
    103, 105
Bridgeton 34
Brigantine Beach 68

C

Camden 113, 128, 129, 133, 136, 138,
141, 143, 144, 149, 160, 162,
168, 172, 174
Camp Kilmer 160
Camp Nordland 158
Camp Voorhees 135
Cape May 11, 18, 27, 69, 85, 117, 118,
126, 160, 161, 164, 170
Caridi, Salvatore 159
Carteret, George 33, 35, 36
Carteret, James 35
Carteret, Philip 36, 37
Closter Horseman 74
Colman, John 17
Cornelius, Titus 77
Cuban Missile Crisis 171
Curtiss-Wright Plant 162

D

de Vries, David 16, 18, 19, 20, 21,
22, 26
Doughty, John 90, 93, 99
Duquesne Spy Ring 159
Dutch 16, 17, 18, 19, 20, 21, 22, 23,
26, 27, 28, 29, 30, 34, 35, 36,
42, 63, 76

E

Easton Conference 59
Edge, Walter Evans 151, 154, 166
Egg Harbor 68, 98, 100, 105
election of 1812 103
election of 1860 118
election of 1864 118
election of 1916 151
Elizabeth 35, 36, 54, 67, 73, 75, 82,
86, 104, 130

F

First Battle of Trenton 80
Forage War 84
Ford, Jacob, Jr. 89

Fort Christina
Fort Christina 20, 26, 27, 28, 29
Fort Dix 151, 155, 160, 161, 163, 168,
172, 177
Fort Hancock 138, 169
Fort Lee 71
Fort Nassau 18, 19, 20, 27
French and Indian War 48, 52, 79, 89,
93
Fries's Rebellion 98

G

Glassboro Summit 174
Glorious Enterprise 43, 44, 46, 47
Glorious Revolution 38
Great Railroad Strike 133
Greenwich Tea Party 67

H

Hackensack 21, 45, 74, 78, 82, 88,
113, 147
Hamilton, Andrew 40
Hancock House Massacre 85
Hercules Powder Plant Disaster 157
Hobart, Garret 134
Hoboken 22, 30, 132, 152, 154, 159, 176
Hoffman, Harold G. 152
Howell, Richard 95, 96, 99
Hudson, Henry 16, 177

J

Jersey Blues 34, 55, 56, 57, 60, 61, 97,
104, 122, 154
Jersey City 21, 30, 86, 128, 132, 133,
135, 145, 158, 163, 172, 174, 176
Johnson, John 60

K

Kearny, Lawrence 111
Kearny, Philip 115, 122
Kearny, Stephen W. 115
Kieft, William 20, 21, 22, 23
Kilpatrick, Hugh Judson 127
King George's War 46

King Philip's War 33
Kingsland Fire 147
Korean War 170
Kosovo War 175

L

Lawrence, James 105
Lenape 13, 15, 16, 56, 59
Liberty Boys 66

M

Massacre of Little Egg Harbor 69
McClellan, George 118, 133
Mercer, Hugh 71, 73
Mexican War 112
Middletown 35, 41, 169
Military Road 54
Millville 161
Morris, Lewis 40, 41, 43, 50
Mulliner, Joe 77

N

National Guard 133, 151, 152, 164,
    170, 171, 174, 175
Navesink 42, 43, 139
Newark 16, 22, 33, 34, 35, 36, 49, 50,
    51, 57, 74, 82, 88, 102, 104,
    107, 112, 115, 118, 121, 127,
    128, 135, 141, 143, 150, 151,
    152, 158, 159, 161, 162, 168,
    172, 174, 176, 177
New Brunswick 59, 75, 79, 82, 84, 94,
    113, 135, 141, 160, 168
New Jersey Battalion of Volunteers
    (Mexican War) 113
New Jersey Land Riots 49
New Jersey Line War 62
New Netherlands 13, 19, 20, 21, 23,
    27, 28, 35
New York Shipbuilding 143, 160,
    162, 168

O

Ogden, Aaron 103
Ogden, Matthias 90
Olden, Charles Smith 118
Old Mine Road 54, 58
Operation Pastorius 159
Operation RAW 173

P

Parker Castle 47
Parker, Joel 118
Paterson 104, 105, 113, 118, 128, 134,
    135, 141, 162, 168, 172, 174
Paulins Kill Raid 56
Paulus Hook 30, 70, 71, 73, 85, 86, 103
Pavonia 21, 22, 30
Peninsula Campaign 122
Perry, Nehemiah 118, 124
Persian Gulf War 175
Perth Amboy 34, 39, 45, 47, 50, 51,
    52, 59, 71, 73, 84, 98, 100, 111,
    127, 149
Pike, Zebulon 95, 106, 110, 112
Piscataway 34, 35, 160
Pompton Lakes 134, 137
Pompton Mutiny 88
Princeton 53, 67, 71, 75, 79, 81, 82,
    84, 99, 100, 115, 118, 152
Princeton Tea Party 66
Printz, Johan 19, 26, 27, 29

Q

Quakers 40, 42, 43, 44, 46, 62, 63, 82,
    90, 103, 172
Quasi War 98
Quebec 44, 56, 104
Queen Anne's War 42, 44, 45, 47

R

Riots of 1871 133
Roberts, Amos 49, 50, 51

Roebling Wire and Cable Plant Fire 144
Rosenberg, Ethel and Julius 167

S

Sandy Hook 16, 28, 42, 43, 45, 47,
    67, 70, 86, 101, 105, 138, 141,
    160, 168
Sayreville 134, 141, 149
Schuyler, Peter 48, 53, 55, 56, 57, 60
Scott, Winfield 109, 110, 113, 115,
    122, 175
Seabrook Farms 163
Sea Girt 135, 139, 152
Second Battle of Trenton 82
Second Seminole War 110
Shrewsbury 22, 35, 40, 70, 76
Siege of Fort Oswego 56
Siege of Fort William Henry 57
Skinner, Cortlandt 76
Somers, Richard 100
South Amboy 149, 169
Stevens Family 132
Stockton, Richard 75
Stockton, Robert F. 115
Stuyvesant, Peter 27, 28, 29, 31, 35
Susquehannock 15, 29, 30
Sussex County fortifications 58
Swartwout family 62
Sweden 16, 20, 26, 27, 28, 29

T

T.A. Gillespie Shell Loading Plant
    Explosion 149
Third Anglo-Dutch War 34
Toms River 68, 89
Tories 76
Trenton 11, 59, 61, 75, 79, 80, 81, 84,
    90, 96, 112, 115, 118, 121, 127,
    128, 132, 144, 152, 175
Trenton Barracks 59
Tripolitan War 100

U

USS *Holland* 141
USS *Maine* 134
USS *Warrior* 109

V

Vietnam War 171
Voorhees, Foster McGowan 134

W

War of 1812 101
War of Jenkins' Ear 45, 46
Washington, George 11, 46, 68, 70, 71,
    73, 74, 75, 78, 79, 80, 81, 82,
    84, 85, 86, 88, 89, 90, 94, 95,
    96, 98, 99, 100, 104, 107, 121,
    138, 154, 161, 173, 176
Westfall family 62
Whiskey Rebellion 95, 98
Woodbridge 34, 35, 78, 84, 95

ABOUT THE AUTHOR

David R. Petriello is a college professor and lifelong resident of New Jersey. He holds a doctorate in modern history. Having taught the history of New Jersey for many years, Dr. Petriello has always been fascinated by the role that the state has played in the larger history of the nation. Other works by the author include *American Prometheus: The Impact of Ronald Reagan upon the Modernization of China* and *From Sea to Syphilitic Sea: The Impact of Disease upon American History*.